D0195532

Dramatists Play Service

OUTSTANDING MEN'S MONOLOGUES 2001–2002

Edited by CRAIG POSPISIL

★

★

DRAMATISTS
PLAY SERVICE
INC.

OUTSTANDING MEN'S MONOLOGUES 2001–2002
Copyright © 2002, Dramatists Play Service, Inc.

All Rights Reserved

INTRODUCTION

There has been a proliferation of monologue collections in recent years. Browse through the theatre section of any bookstore and you will find collections of dramatic monologues, comic ones, classical ones; monologues written by men, by women, by gay writers, Asian-American writers, African-American writers, the best monologues of 1998, 1999, 2000 … you get the idea.

What I noticed was that most of these collections featured the work of authors published by Dramatists Play Service, and so the idea came to me, "Why not a monologue collection drawn solely from plays that we publish?" After all, we represent some of the best of today's playwrights, authors who in the last eight years have won six Pulitzer Prizes and six Tony Awards, authors whose work is produced all across North America and the world, and writers of every stripe and style.

I read through all of the plays that we published in the last couple of seasons and compiled two collections: *Outstanding Men's Monologues 2001–2002* and *Outstanding Women's Monologues 2001–2002*. Each of these books contains over fifty monologues. You will find an enormous range of voices and subject matter, characters from their teens to their seventies and authors from widely varied backgrounds, some well known, others less so, but all immensely talented.

I hope this collection will prove useful to you in your search for audition material, classroom work or just for reading pleasure. Perhaps you'll be introduced to some new authors as well. I know you'll find some very exciting writing for the theatre in these pages.

Craig Pospisil
New York City
October 2001

CONTENTS

4

AMONG FRIENDS

BY KRISTINE THATCHER

WILL — mid to late 40s, a teacher of English in a Chicago public high school.

SYNOPSIS: Three old friends, Matt and brothers-in-law Will and Dan, gather as often as possible to play poker. Matt is a struggling Sears appliance salesman; Will, a public school teacher; and Dan, a real-estate developer and award-winning humanitarian. Dan is by far the most successful of the three and appears to be a model citizen. But when Will surreptitiously discovers the lionized Dan cheating at cards, he decides to explore exactly how deeply the rot goes. AMONG FRIENDS plumbs the nature of friendship, and the jealousy and resentment that sometimes lie just beneath the surface.

WILL.   Believe it or not, my father and I used to be very close. And the best times we ever had were when we were trolling the east end of that stupid little lake. We had a very private falling-out years ago, before you came into the picture. I thought we could have healed some of the wounds by now, but ...
[DAN.   But what?]
WILL.   You came into the picture. Dad is big on service. You serve your country, no ifs, ands, or buts. Well, he was on the first minesweeper that entered the harbor of Hiroshima twenty-two days after we dropped the bomb. That's what all his skin cancer is about, don't you think?
[DAN.   Maybe.]
WILL.   He told me Hiroshima was leveled as far as the eye could see. It looked like a junkyard. Those who survived were starving. Parents offered their daughters in exchange for food. A number of his shipmates bought and used these children for the price of a

7

Hershey bar. That was profound for him. Hell, it's profound for me, and I heard about it secondhand. *(Pause.)* Hearing that turned me into a confirmed pacifist. But not Dad. He understood something I'll never understand. But *you* understand it. You two are in the same club. You share the same sense of patriotism and duty, the same resolution. Do you think a man like Dad could possibly be proud of his son, the draft-dodger? Nobody gives you a medal for founding your local SDS chapter, or writing for the underground, or holding the line when the National Guard arrives on campus. He always taught me to stand up for my principles, no matter what; that if I did that, he would always be proud of me. But when I did just that, I lost him. So, after I graduated, I didn't go to L.A. I followed my father into teaching. And I might have gotten him back, but then you came along. When you married Diane, he finally got his war hero son.

BLESSED ASSURANCE

BY LADDY SARTIN

SLICK — a troubled young white man, grew up in the community and around the café, actually has a touch of the poet, but it has long been beaten down by his kinsmen.

SYNOPSIS: It is the turbulent Freedom Summer of 1964. Olivia, the African-American cook for the Whitehouse Café, has shocked her small southern town by marching up the courthouse steps demanding to register to vote. Because of this she is attacked from all sides, even by those closest to her heart. Slick lectures her. Harlan, the owner of the café, who is like a son to Olivia, accuses her of listening to outside agitators and following along "like cows being led to slaughter." This damnation incites Olivia to challenge Harlan's personal beliefs, and his allegiance to her, by sitting at the counter of the café where she has worked most of her life and requesting to be served. When Harlan asks her what she thinks she's doing, she says "I think they call it a sit-in!" Olivia's choice to stand up for her rights forces the people close to her to confront the hatred, ignorance and injustice of the town.

SLICK. Come on over here so you can hear me. Take all day, ain't nothing gonna change. Are you listening to me? Hey? Come on. I been sent here to tell you how things are gonna be. In my heart I don't want none of this. You know that, don't you? You know why they sent me? Huh? Well, what? You ain't got nothing to say? Why couldn't you just stay in your place? You never done nothing like this before. Most folks, people in town, always thought of you as good colored. You know what they saying now, you know what the word is out on you? That you been listening to outside agitators. You stand there and stare at me like I done wrong, but it's you! It was you! You don't know your place. What would you think if I drove out to the country club and stood around knocking on the front door whining about somebody letting me in? They ain't gonna let me be no member of the country club. You see what I mean? What if I drove over to the Jews' synagogue and tried to get in? Ain't no way they gonna let me in, 'cause they know and I know I ain't no Jew. It ain't my place. So what in God's name do you think you doing romping around the courthouse? Huh?

BLUES FOR AN ALABAMA SKY

BY PEARL CLEAGE

GUY JACOBS — a 30-ish black man; costume designer at the Cotton Club.

SYNOPSIS: It is the summer of 1930 in Harlem, New York. The creative euphoria of the Harlem Renaissance has given way to the harsher realities of the Great Depression. The play brings together a rich cast of characters who reflect the conflicting currents of the time through their overlapping personalities and politics. Set in the Harlem apartment of Guy, a popular costume designer, and his friend, Angel, a recently fired Cotton Club back-up singer, the cast also includes Sam, a hard-working, jazz-loving doctor at Harlem Hospital; Delia, an equally dedicated member of the staff at the Sanger clinic; and Leland, a recent transplant from Tuskegee, who sees in Angel a memory of lost love and a reminder of those "Alabama skies where the stars are so thick it's bright as day." But Angel doesn't want to be Leland's dream.

GUY.   When I first met Angel at Miss Lillie's, she was already saving her getaway money. She had the little coins and crumpled-up dollar bills all knotted up in somebody's great big silk handkerchief. She was headed up to Harlem as fast as she could get there and she believed it so hard, I believed it, too. So I got my own white silk handkerchief and started putting those coins in there every day and counting them every night. And I'd be lying there with my eyes closed, letting those old men touch me wher-

11

ever they felt like it, but it didn't matter, because in my mind, I was stomping at the Savoy! But I never told Angel. I just kept my ears open so when she was ready to make a move, I'd be ready too. One of the other girls told me she was leaving one night late, so I got my little suitcase and met her at the train station. She was happy to see me, but she sure would have left without me. *(A beat.)* Angel doesn't like to say good-bye.

BOOK OF DAYS

BY LANFORD WILSON

EARL HILL — 34, a big man. Dairy inspector at the cheese plant.

SYNOPSIS: All seems right in Dublin, Missouri. Ruth Hoch has just been cast as the lead in the local production of St. Joan, *and she has her hands full between memorizing her lines and her bookkeeping job. She relies on Len, her husband, and Martha, her iconoclastic mother-in-law, for support. But when Ruth's boss, and Dublin's most prominent citizen, dies in a hunting accident, she senses that something isn't right. The story that Earl tells about the night of the accident has too many loose ends, and Ruth cannot stop pulling at the threads even though it may turn the whole town against her.*

EARL.   I swear to God it looked like the storm was letting up. We'd been planning this for over a month. I come up to the back door, I thought, He's not going to be up, he'll have chickened out and gone back to bed with this rain. I was already gettin' pissed he hadn't called me, save me from coming over. I knocked real light on the back door — hell, he was up and dressed, had a thermos of coffee made, rarin' to go.

I swear it looked like the storm had passed, we thought it was over. It was starting to get light out. Then by the time we got out to the lake, it started getting darker and darker, we got out of the truck, walked to the blind with Walt's flashlight, it started raining like I don't remember ever seeing rain before; you couldn't see your hand in front of your face. And the wind, goddamn, I never been in a wind like that.

And then she comes. Goddamn. Barreling down like a freight-train. Oh, Jesus. We couldn't see a goddamned thing, but Walt and me both knew what it was. Walt had his mouth right in my ear, yellin', Lay down flat and hang on to something. My ears were poppin', chest about to explode from the change in pressure. You never hear about that, no one had ever told me about that. I took the sheriff out to see the place. The track it left was, the sheriff said, almost a quarter of a mile wide, twelve miles long. It had taken every tree, every bit of underbrush, every blade of grass right down to the mud. You could see how the actual twister missed us by about thirty feet. But it had downed a lot of trees around where Walt and me was. Walt must have been twisted around, disoriented. Goddamn was he strong. You could see where he had crawled maybe ten feet. He had his shotgun there, under him, and he was down under the branches of this oak, you couldn't tell if the tree got him first or his gun did. Sheriff said it looked like the tree pushed him, got him off balance, caused him to twist the gun around. God, Len, his chest, part of his face, is just gone. Sharon can no way have an open casket.

THE BUNGLER

BY JEAN BAPTISTE POQUELIN
DE MOLIÈRE

Translated into English by Richard Wilbur

MASCARILLE — (mah-ska-REE), Lélie's valet.

SYNOPSIS: THE BUNGLER takes place in the Sicilian city of Messina. A beautiful young woman named Célie has been traveling with a gypsy band and has been left by them with a rich old man named Trufaldin as security for a loan. Two young men of Messina, Lélie and Léandre, have been rivals for the hand of a girl named Hippolyte, but when Célie appears on the scene they are smitten by her, and she becomes the new object of their rivalry. The warm, impetuous Lélie turns to his valet, a cunning trickster named Mascarille, for help in outwitting Léandre and in freeing the pawned Célie. Mascarille, who loves to plot and deceive, contrives ruse after ruse in his master's interest, but is repeatedly frustrated by the blunders of Lélie — who manages unintentionally to spoil them. As the result of certain discoveries, the play is able at its close to unite Lélie with his Célie, who turns out to be of gentle birth. Léandre is reunited with Hippolyte, to the satisfaction of her father, Anselme, and indeed the dénouement pleases everyone, including Trufaldin. It is, as Mascarille observes, "like the ending of a comedy."

MASCARILLE.
Hush, my good nature; you haven't a grain of sense,
And I'll no longer hear your arguments.
It's you, my anger, that I'll listen to.
Am I obliged forever to undo
The blunders of a clod? I should resign!

15

That fool has spoiled too many schemes of mine.
And yet, let's think about this matter coolly.
Were I to let my just impatience rule me,
They'd say that I'd been quick to call it quits,
And that I'd lost the vigor of my wits;
And what then would become of my renown
As the most glorious trickster in the town,
A reputation that I've earned by never
Failing to think of something wildly clever?
O Mascarille, let honor be your guide!
Persist in those great works which are your pride,
And though your master irks you, persevere
Not for his sake, but for your own career.
Yet what can you accomplish, when the force
Of a demonic head wind blocks your course,
And you're compelled to tack and tack again?
What is the use of persevering, when
His folly brings continual heavy weather,
And sinks the best schemes you can put together?
Well, out of kindness, let us give it one
Final attempt, and see what can be done;
Then, if he wrecks our chances as before,
I swear that I'll not help him anymore.
We might, in fact, accomplish our desire
If we could get our rival to retire —
If, backing off, Léandre would allow
Me one whole day for the plot I'm hatching now.
Yes, I'm now thinking out an artful plan
Which surely will succeed, if I but can
Remove the obstacle I've spoken of.
He's coming: I'll test the firmness of his love.

CHICKEN POTENTIAL

From FOOD RELATED in the collection
OREGON AND OTHER SHORT PLAYS

BY PETER HEDGES

ZEKE — a young man.

SYNOPSIS: While cooking some eggs, Guy considers the merits of various women as potential girlfriends, but his friend, Zeke, shoots down every option, listing a host of physical or psychological problems for each one.

ZEKE. Hey. Hey! You obviously aren't seeing things clearly here. You live, my friend, in a land where opportunity abounds. Some people aren't given a chance at this life. Some people call Cambodia home. Some people died in wars, ate grenades for breakfast. Some guys are prevented but Guy — what is preventing you, pray tell? At least you were born! At least you got vaccinated! AT LEAST YOU WERE TAUGHT TO LOOK BOTH WAYS! AT LEAST THEY CIRCUMCISED IT WHEN YOU WERE A BABY! DO YOU KNOW WHAT IT FEELS LIKE WHEN THEY DO IT TO A GROWN-UP GUY, GUY?! AT LEAST YOU WERE BORN WHITE MALE! IT'S A WHITE MALE WORLD AND IT IS YOURS! AT LEAST YOU PREFER GIRLS! YOU DON'T HAVE NO HAIR LIP, NO BIRTH MARK, NO TOOTH CAPPED IN SILVER! WHAT MORE DO YOU WANT?! *(Pause.)* I think about all the places, all the people and I remember Chad Simms. He hated America. He knew it was better elsewhere. So he defected. He quit it all. Chad Simms is a commie now. But there are no commies anymore, if you think about it. Now he wants back in. I got a postcard last week. He wants to live in America again. See? See what I'm saying? I had a barber named Ramirez. Now you know what Ramirez is. He isn't you or me. He is a Mexican American, a wetback, my Sancho Panza. What a guy. He cut my hair. In America — he was allowed to cut my hair. Do not go knocking your country.

CLOSER

BY PATRICK MARBER

LARRY — a man from the city.

SYNOPSIS: Four lives intertwine over the course of four and a half years. Dan, an obituary writer, meets Alice, a stripper, after an accident in the street. Eighteen months later, they are a couple, and Dan has written a novel inspired by her. While posing for his book jacket cover, Dan meets Anna, a photographer. He pursues her, but she rejects his advances despite their mutual attraction. Larry, a dermatologist, "meets" Dan in an Internet chat room. Dan, obsessing over Anna, pretends to be her and has cybersex with Larry. They arrange to meet the next day at an aquarium. Larry arrives and so too, coincidentally, does the real Anna. This sets up a series of pass-the-lover scenes in which this quartet struggle to find intimacy, but can't seem to get closer.

LARRY.   Ever *seen* a human heart? It looks like a fist wrapped in blood.
  GO FUCK YOURSELF … you … <u>*WRITER*</u>. You <u>LIAR</u>.
  Go check a few facts while I get my hands dirty.
[DAN.   She hates your hands. She hates your simplicity.]
(Pause.)
LARRY.   <u>Listen</u> … I've spent the whole week talking about *you*.
  Anna tells me you fucked her with your eyes closed.
  She tells me you wake in the night, crying for your dead mother.
  You mummy's boy.
  Shall we stop this?
  It's *over*. Accept it.
  You don't know the first thing about love because you don't understand *compromise*.

19

You don't even know ... *Alice.*
Consider her scar, how did she get that?
(Beat.)
[DAN. When did you meet Alice?]
(Pause.)
LARRY. Anna's exhibition. *You* remember.
A scar in the shape of a question mark, solve the mystery.
[DAN. She got it when her parents' car crashed.]
(Pause.)
LARRY. There's a condition called *"Dermatitis Artefacta."* It's a mental disorder manifested in the skin. The patient manufactures his or her very own skin disease. They pour bleach on themselves, gouge their skin, inject themselves with their own piss, sometimes their own shit. They create their own disease with the same diabolical attention to detail as the artist or the lover. It looks "real" but its source is the deluded self.
I think Alice mutilated herself.
It's fairly common in children who lose their parents young.
They blame themselves, they're disturbed.
[DAN. Alice is not "disturbed."]
LARRY. *[But she is.]*
You were so busy feeling your grand artistic *"feelings"* you couldn't see what was in front of you. The girl is fragile and tender. She didn't want to be put in a book, she wanted to be *loved.*

THE COUNTESS

BY GREGORY MURPHY

JOHN RUSKIN — 35, preeminent nineteenth-century art critic.

SYNOPSIS: Based on one of the most notorious scandals of the Victorian Age, THE COUNTESS is a true account of madness, cruelty and obsession, and perhaps one of the greatest love stories of its time. In 1853, preeminent art critic John Ruskin, his wife, Effie, and his friend and protégé, the Pre-Raphaelite painter John Everett Millais, depart in high spirits for the Scottish Highlands. When they return to London four months later, Millais' hatred for Ruskin is exceeded only by his passion for the beautiful, young Mrs. Ruskin. What John Everett Millais did not know — could not have known — was the terrible truth at the core of the Ruskin marriage. A secret which when revealed through the persistence of Lady Elizabeth Eastlake, renowned writer of the period and close friend of Effie Ruskin, would rock London society and forever change the lives of Millais and the Ruskins.

RUSKIN. Frank will be some time getting the carriage, so you might as well sit and wait. *(Effie paces nervously.)* Take your ease, Mrs. Ruskin, you will be free of me soon enough. *(Effie sits down. Ruskin notices her luggage.)* Two little bags. How like you, Effie. Do you think I don't know about the trunks you've sent to Bowerswell. Trunks for a three-month stay. *(Effie stiffens slightly.)* Is there someone in Scotland for you to captivate — Millais perhaps — is that why you're so keen to be off, or is it you plan to give your sisters a fashion show with their lesson? *(Ruskin, noticing Effie is nervously preoccupied, pauses a moment.)* Effie, when you return in August from Bowerswell you had better regained what little self-composure you had. *(Pause.)* These fits of fretfulness. Your irri-

tability and sullenness these past few days have been intolerable. You will change, Mrs. Ruskin, and return, if not the affectionate, tractable wife I'd once hoped, then at least a calmer, less distracting one. *(Effie turns and stares at her husband with a look of absolute hatred.)* Do you think I care you despise me? Do you? Answer me. [EFFIE. *(Murmuring.)* God, be with me.]
RUSKIN. What was that you said? What? *(Effie does not respond.)* Answer me! Answer me! *(Effie does not respond.)* Nothing at all. Mad. My wife is mad. *(Pause.)* Wife? She is not a wife. A wife gives comfort to her husband. Not a creator of discord between her husband and his parents. Wife? Did she tend to her husband's needs? Help him in his work? Did she once suffer to keep her opinions to herself? Wife? Did she ever seek to soothe rather than irritate, pacify rather than engage, or to be unassuming and modest instead of proud.
[EFFIE. *You dare ask what kind of wife I've been? You, who have sought to degrade and compromise me in any and every way you could. Who have tried to rob me of my dignity — my very reason.*
RUSKIN. *It isn't so.*
EFFIE. *I'm trying not to hate you, John.*
RUSKIN. *Hate me?*
EFFIE. *I pray God keep me from hating you.]*
RUSKIN. You hardly know what you say. Your mind grows weaker and more disorganised daily. Yes. As your body sickens and corrupts. *(Effie rises quickly.)*
[EFFIE. Crawley! *(Ruskin flies at his wife, taking her by the arm.)]*
RUSKIN. I will break you, Effie.

THE COUNTRY CLUB

BY DOUGLAS CARTER BEANE

BRI — for Brian. Married to Froggy and not originally from Wyomissing. Bespectacled and well-groomed. Despite being so well assembled, he always seems a little uncomfortable.

SYNOPSIS: Soos, young, witty and charmingly neurotic, retreats from a failed marriage to her upper-class hometown. The type of WASP domain with the houses "that made Martha Stewart forget she was Polish." As party after party unfolds, the getaway weekend gives way to a year, and ultimately the rest of her life. Brittle conversation is bandied about, and Soos is reunited with her onetime boyfriend, the ever charming Zip. She also returns to her circle of old friends: the highly strung party planner Froggy, the wry and sarcastic Pooker and the drunken good ol' boy Hutch. But cracks soon begin to show in the veneer. Zip falls in and out of an easy relationship with Soos. He starts an affair with Chloe, Hutch's nouveau wife. They soon discover, however, that the affair is widely know even if not widely talked about. Lives are casually destroyed and lives go on.

BRI.   Shit. Another thing we're too late for. How many times does that happen, right?
[POOKER.   What?]
BRI.   Something important happens and we're too late for it. It's like everything that's important has happened before us. I feel that I was late for the Sixties. Just being born and all. Protesting and shit? I would have done it. I would have been a real, you know, vigorous rebel against Vietnam. I would have hated Vietnam. I would have carried a sign. No sweat. If there were a Vietnam-like situation today, I would protest. I would sing songs with a guitar. Grow my hair long. Make peace signs. And just, you know ... hate

the establishment and stuff. Where's the dip?

[ZIP.   Aren't there Vietnam-like situations now?

BRI.   *I don't think so. I think we'd know about it.*

ZIP.   Brian, we've invaded quite a few countries since Vietnam.]

BRI.   [Yes, but] wars now are so short. By the time you figure out which side you're on, they're long over. I mean Vietnam was long enough to be so black and white. You knew what to be angry about. Wars now are like bright gray. The really good angry is gone.

[POOKER.   Civil rights, like.]

BRI.   Exactly. Civil rights. Case in fucking point. I would have been a champion of civil rights. Separate counters and such? Oh I would have been so against it, it wouldn't even be funny. I would have marched with Martin Luther ... King. But all that's ... said and done. I mean there is inequality and stuff all over the world. Racial whatnot. I'm not blind. But it's all over there. In ... whattayacall?

[FROGGY.   Kosovo. Pass the nuts.]

BRI.   Kosovo. It's none of our business. For protest and rage and stuff? We're just too late. Face it.

COYOTE ON A FENCE

BY BRUCE GRAHAM

BOBBY REYBURN — in his late 20s, skinny, pale.

SYNOPSIS: Illiterate but likable, Bobby Reyburn is a funny young guy who loves to do impressions. He's also a member of the Aryan nation, a racist predator convicted of a horrific crime. John Brennan is educated and arrogant, a serious writer who may only be guilty of doing society a favor. Sam Fried is a reporter who is writing an article on John for the New York Times. *As he interviews people at the prison, he challenges John's claim of innocence and shows that the divide between John and Bobby may not be so great after all.*

BOBBY. So my mother — the whore — I tell 'er wanta go to Uncle Hew's but she — heck — she couldn't got me there if she wanted to and this man's she with, he ... so I walked — *(Laughs.)* Well, limped. Six miles outta town — man-oh-man it hurt — didn't have no aspirin or nothin'. Just wanted to get to my uncle's and I'm gettin' close I can see the lights out there and ... man-oh-man, almost peed myself — 'cause there's this ... monster! And it's floatin' in the air there, and I can see its eyes and — *(Laughs.)* Well, lemme tell ya, John: If there was a limpin' race in the Olympics, I'd of won it that night. I burst in on poor Hew shakin' and cryin' and heck — he didn't even know I was comin' but he hugged me there and put me in the truck and drove on out there. Coyote — that's all it was — stuck up on the barbed wire there. I figure it got caught in the fence till ol' Hew showed me the bullet hole. He'd shot it and stuck it up there. Beat on it too, while it was wounded. So we went back, he fed me, put me ta bed — but he sees I'm still upset 'bout it. Ya know how kids don't wanta see any

25

animal get hurt. So he sat there onna bed and told me 'bout coyotes bein' evil and predators and how it's okay ta kill 'em and there's nothin' to he ashamed of. That's why he stuck it up onna fence there. Let the world know — death to predators. *(Simply.)* Then he told me all about the Jews. How Hitler knew they were predators and about the cabal and everything. How they was usin' the niggers and mud people to turn us all into animals so they can enslave us. *(Laughs sadly, remembering.)* Uncle Hew, he had a beautiful voice. Coulda been on the radio. So, couple days later, he takes me out to Mr. George's — 'member him, the bike guy? Terrence George, George Terrence? Well he had this big garage like out in the middle of the woods. Musta been a hundred people there: old, young, babies feedin' on their moms and ... and Mr. George calls me up to the front there and asks if I'll swear my allegiance. And I say "sure" and so we do it and ... John, I look back and ol' Hew, he's smilin'. He's so proud'a me. And I walk down the aisle there ... And, John, they all reached out. Shakin' my hand, pattin' me on the back ... huggin' me ... *(Savoring it.)* Ol' Hew beamin' back there and all this ... love. They was reachin' out for me, John. Reachin' out ... You make peace with yourself, John. And write anything ya want 'bout me. Don't matter. I am a lucky man, John. A lucky man ...

A DEVIL INSIDE

BY DAVID LINDSAY-ABAIRE

BRAD — in his mid-30s, a ridiculously plain man who longs for something more than the appliance repair shop that he runs.

SYNOPSIS: Mrs. Slater has waited fourteen long years to tell her son, Gene, the truth. And when he wakes up on his twenty-first birthday, she tells him, "Your father was murdered. He was stabbed in the back and his feet were lopped off and thrown into a drainage ditch." Gene would rather focus his attentions on Caitlin, a passionate literature major, than avenge the death of his 400-pound father. Caitlin barely notices Gene and is herself obsessed with her Russian Lit professor, a tormented genius who thinks he's living in a Dostoyevsky novel. Suddenly, a mysterious woman named Lily stumbles into the family-owned laundromat, and is instantly struck by the pain etched into Mrs. Slater's face. Lily, in turn, is living with Brad, an absurdly dull appliance repairman who has taken to writing children's stories to jazz up his boring life, which gets progressively and horrifyingly thrilling the further he gets pulled into the unraveling events.

BRAD. I didn't know what to do. So Satan taught me how to hot-wire the van. My first thought was to get away, but the FDR was closed, so I drove west and took the Holland Tunnel to New Jersey, but there were cracks in it. And I thought this can't be right. I mean, the Hudson River was dribbling its way into the Holland Tunnel. And when I got out, I pulled off into a parking lot to contemplate exactly what was going on, and I could see across the river to the city, and cars were sliding off of the West Side Highway, just disappearing into the Hudson. And Satan was in the passenger's seat telling me to keep driving, to head south and forget about it, get out while I could. And I was saying something

27

back to him, when a New York City cop tapped on the driver's side window and said, "Who you talking to there, buddy boy?" And I couldn't figure out what a New York cop was doing in New Jersey, but I said, "It's Satan, officer. He floated off of my wallpaper and made me steal this van which crippled a boy." At that point I was dragged out of my vehicle and for the first time took a good look around. The parking lot was filled with New York City police cars, hundreds of them, and garbage trucks, public works vans, fire trucks, and off in the distance was a huge warehouse and there were tractor trailers pulling in shipments, handing them off to men in uniform, vats of hot coffee, crates of warm crullers. So I yelled at the cop, "What the hell is going on here?" And he started beating me with a club, and four or five other cops came waddling over and joined in, kicked me and beat me and threw donuts at my head until I couldn't move. And then they headed back to the warehouse, stuffing their bloated faces with jelly rolls. So I dragged myself to the van, started it up, and ran them down. They never had a chance. They were too fat to run. Sure, they could drag me into court, but they couldn't do anything because Satan video-taped the whole beating. *(Pulls out video.)* Those sons of bitches. So I ripped it out of there and started back to the city, thinking they'd never follow me, but they did. The entire NYPD leapt into their cars and followed me into the leaking tunnel, except by that time the cracks were bigger and the water was rushing in. I hydroplaned the whole way through, with hundreds of cop cars on my tail, blaring their sirens. I felt like the Pope. Sections of tunnel were caving in behind me, water filling the place. The minute I flew up and out, the river kicked in. The Hudson came crashing down, flooding the Holland Tunnel and the entire NYPD as if the waters were the parted Red Sea falling in on the Egyptian Army, and I was Moses, safe on the other side with my people.

THE DIARY OF ANNE FRANK

BY FRANCES GOODRICH AND ALBERT HACKETT

NEWLY ADAPTED BY WENDY KESSELMAN

OTTO FRANK — Anne's father.

SYNOPSIS: It is World War II and Amsterdam has fallen to the Nazi regime. Seeking refuge in a forgotten storage attic, Otto and Edith Frank try to maintain a sense of security and hope for their daughters, Margot and Anne. With limited supplies, they agree to hide another family, the van Daans, and a dentist, Mr. Dussel. Days become months as tensions mount and news reports worsen. Anne, a gifted young girl of fourteen, records the daily events in her diary. Her accounts are filled with the humor, pain and passion of a young girl becoming a woman. She tries to maintain her belief in the general goodness of humanity, but as her world and traditions are destroyed, her optimism fades. The families survive bitter winters, malnutrition and volatile relationships, but they are ultimately captured.

MR. FRANK. Westerbork. A barren heath. Wooden towers where our jailers stand guard. Walls covered with thousands of flies. The eight of us crammed into Prison Barrack 67 — betrayed. We never know by whom. Our last month together. Anne and Peter walking hand in hand between the barracks and barbed wire. Edith worrying about the children, washing underclothing in murky water, numb. Margot, silent, staring at nothing. Our last days on Dutch soil. Late August, Paris freed. Brussels. Antwerp. But for us it is too late. Tuesday September third, 1944, a thousand of us herded into cattle cars, the last transport to leave

29

Westerbork for the extermination camps. *(He pauses.)*
The train. Three days, three nights. In the middle of the third night ... Auschwitz. Separation. Men from women. Edith. Margot. Anne. My family. Never again. Selection. Half our transport killed in the gas chambers. One day Peter and I see a group of men march away, his father among them. Gassed. Peter on the "death march" to Mauthausen. Dead three days before the British arrive. His mother — Auschwitz, Bergen-Belsen, Buchenwald, Theresienstadt — date of death unknown. Mr. Dussel dies in Neuengamme. *(Pause.)*
January twenty-seventh, 1945. I am freed from Auschwitz. I know nothing of Edith and the children. And then I learn ... Edith died in Birkenau of grief, hunger, exhaustion. *(Pause.)*
The winter of '45, typhus breaks out in Bergen-Belsen, killing thousands of prisoners, among them Margot. Anne's friend, Hanneli, sees Anne through the barbed wire, naked, her head shaved, covered with lice. "I don't have anyone anymore," she weeps. A few days later, Anne dies. My daughters' bodies dumped into mass graves, just before the camp is liberated. *(Mr. Frank bends down, picks up Anne's diary lying on the floor. He steps forward, the diary in his hands.)* All that remains.

DIMINISHED CAPACITY

BY TOM DULACK

TROY — 51, somewhat haggard.

SYNOPSIS: Judge Frank Troy is a burned-out New York State Supreme Court judge. On the morning after his father dies, he finds himself arguing with his young law student summer intern, and fending off his sister on the phone who is trying to persuade him to attend his father's funeral, though he never really liked him much. Judge Troy has a particularly vicious criminal ready to come before him for sentencing, and a full calendar to clear in an upcoming session with an Assistant District Attorney and a Legal Aid defender. In the mix comes a request from an old colleague, Duncan, to intervene with the D.A. on behalf of a wealthy client who just threw his wife out of a twenty-five-story window, while in a state of "diminished capacity" after drinking. Judge Troy sympathizes, as he keeps a bottle of vodka in his desk, and uses it. Near it, he also keeps a revolver, which comes into use when the criminal he's about to sentence takes Judge Troy and his intern hostage in the judge's chambers.

TROY.   Friday night some friends were in from Connecticut, from Roxbury, do you know Jeff and Marianna? No, you don't know them. He's a writer. Anyway, we were coming back from Jersey where we had dinner, and we were coming off the West Side Highway at 56th, where you have to stop for the light. And there were these kids, this wolf pack of black extortionists swarming all over the cars stopped for the light, smearing a greasy rag across the windshield — you know, that sense of menace and threat, ill-defined, shapeless, never-stand-up-in-court latent violence, suddenly swarming all over us, and the sense of being trapped, victimized, locked in our expensive German-made driving machine,

31

like in a cage, or in a diving bell, like we'd gone down too deep, and the pressure was cracking the welds, and the seams, and out the portholes were all these carnivores flashing their teeth.
[DUNCAN. What happened?]
TROY. *[Nothing.]* Jeff was driving. One of the kids approached, the light was endless, seemed endless, and Jeff rolled down the window and told him to fuck off.
[DUNCAN. And so he smeared his greasy rag on the windshield anyway, right?]
TROY. No, he didn't do anything. He just walked away, but so insolent, with this strange kind of infuriating, almost seductive insolence. And ... *(He stops, shakes his head at a terrible memory.)*
[DUNCAN. And what, Frank?]
TROY. For a moment, just for a split second, I wanted to kill him. I wanted to kill all of them.

DINNER WITH FRIENDS

BY DONALD MARGULIES

GABE — in his 40s.

SYNOPSIS: Karen and Gabe invited their best friends, Beth and Tom, over for dinner. Beth arrives without Tom, making excuses for him, but she soon breaks down into tears and admits that Tom has left her for another woman. Karen and Gabe are nearly as shocked as Beth. They had long envisioned a lovely future, growing old alongside their friends, watching each other's children marry. Later that night as Beth is getting ready for bed Tom shows up at their home and is angered when he learns Beth already told Karen and Gabe the news. He and Beth had agreed to tell them together. Sure that Karen now has the "advantage," Tom hurries over to see Karen and Gabe and explain his side of the story. The second act begins at a dinner twelve years earlier at which the recently married Karen and Gabe introduce Tom and Beth to one another and set their relationship in motion. Back in the present, Karen and Gabe meet with Beth and Tom separately. The two of them seem happier than ever, with new lovers and positive outlooks for the future. But that night as they lie next to each other in bed talking, Karen and Gabe are still unsettled. They have lost their friends forever, and their vision of the future now feels uncertain.

GABE. But it's not that simple, Tom. We were there. Karen and Danny and Isaac and I, we were all there, we were all a big part of that terrible life you had to get the hell away from. Isaac's totally freaked out by this, by the way. So when you repudiate your entire adult life ...
[TOM. *That's not what I've done ...*]
GABE. That's *essentially* what you've done. And I can understand how you might find it necessary to do that: It must be strangely

exhilarating blowing everything to bits.
[TOM. Gabe ...]
GABE. I mean it. You build something that's precarious in even the best of circumstances and you succeed, or at least you make it *look* like you've succeeded, your *friends* think you have, you had *us* fooled, and then, one day, you blow it all up! It's like, I watch Danny and Isaac sometimes, dump all their toys on the floor, Legos and blocks and train tracks, and build these elaborate cities together. They'll spend hours at it, they'll plan and collaborate, and squabble and negotiate, but they'll do it. And then what do they do? They wreck it! No pause to revel in what they accomplished, no sigh of satisfaction, they just launch into a full-throttle attack, bombs bursting, and tear the whole damn thing apart.

EASTER

BY WILL SCHEFFER

MATTHEW RANSOM — 30s; trusting, bighearted, not very clever.

SYNOPSIS: It is Good Friday. Matthew and Wilma have just set up home in Prattsville, Kansas. Wilma had been burning churches in Oklahoma, forcing the couple to flee across the prairie states as felons. Matthew is hopeful he can make things right for them in Kansas with a new home and a steady job. Enter Herman, a violin-playing plumber with enormous feet and angel-like qualities, who fixes the couple's sink, only to discover an Easter egg clogging the pipes. Wilma believes the egg is a sign that she is pregnant. Wilma thanks Herman by washing his feet with her hair. Meanwhile, the town handyman, Zaddock, has been having religious visions of his own. Upon meeting Matthew, Zaddock recognizes him as one the of the individuals responsible for a church burning in their area. Matthew takes Zaddock hostage and reveals the story of his and Wilma's first baby, who died in childbirth, and of Wilma's quest for redemption. When Matthew returns to the cabin Wilma tries to introduce him to Herman, but Matthew can't see him. Matthew confronts Wilma with her delusion and "shoots" Herman, forcing Wilma to relive the event that was the cause of their estrangement and of her intense pain. It is a catharsis long overdue, and Wilma and Matthew must face an uncertain future and begin to rebuild their lives.

MATTHEW. Well, at this time we were livin' in a small house, way outside of town, and in those next few months my business started slackin' off a bit, and I was feelin' a little upset about it and all. The bills were piling up and I guess I was drinkin' a little too much. My car wasn't in good shape and Wilma kept tellin' me to take it in to the garage, but I didn't have the money. One day they turned off the telephone. I got so pissed off I put my hand through the window. Me and Wilma had a little fight and I went out to a bar. When I come back she was washin' out her hair in the sink. It was about a month before the baby was due. She didn't even look at me when I came in, just kept washin' her hair. I was about to say I was sorry when all of a sudden she turned. She screamed out a little. She was holdin' her belly. I asked her what was wrong — and she started to say somethin', but before the words could come she screamed out again and a splash of blood hit the linoleum underneath her like paint. I ran to her and she kind of fell into my arms. I didn't know what to do. I lay her down on the floor and wrapped her in a blanket. I ran out to start up the car, but it wouldn't turn over. From inside the house I heard her screamin'. I ran back inside and when I got there I saw two little legs comin' out of her. Two little legs and feet and they were kickin' ... movin' ... blood everywhere. Oh my God I think I'm gonna be sick ... I carried her to the hospital. Carried her in my arms those two miles. For a while the legs kept kickin' but by the time I got her there ... they had stopped. Doctor said she was lucky to be alive. Said it was the worst birth he'd ever seen. Next day when Wilma woke up, they brought the little dead thing into the room and let her hold it in her arms. She called it Herman. She wouldn't stop talkin' to it. All that day she wouldn't let it go. And when I finally got it away from her she screamed and screamed at me. Hospital let me take it home — you know — to bury it. They gave it to me in a plastic bag. It was so ... little. And later that day, when I was alone, I held it too. I held him in my arms. *(Pause.)* I tried to — to help her forget, to make it be like we were. But somewhere — I think she stopped lovin' me. *(Pause.)* That's the whole of it. The whole story. You want it? You can have it.

THE EROS TRILOGY

BY NICKY SILVER

PHILIP — a young man fraught with anxiety.

SYNOPSIS: THE EROS TRILOGY is a collection of three short, the-matically related pieces, CLAIRE, PHILIP and ROGER & MIRIAM. In PHILIP, Claire's son, addresses the audience. Stylistically he is her polar opposite, a mass of anxiety and tension, who lives a life without intimacy or human contact. Fearful and full of self-loathing, Philip becomes fixated on a young man whose name he doesn't know. Terrified of rejection, he lives his life for furtive glances. Finally con-quering his fear, he attempts to make contact — an act of bravery that leads to a terrifying and violent result.

PHILIP. Philip and Girls:
     When I was thirteen years old I had my first sexual experience. I don't mean I had sex. I had my first sexual experience. I KNOW! That's the same thing. I mean, I had an experience of a sexual nature with another person, which is more than a lot of people ever have. I didn't penetrate or anything. I didn't actually ejaculate at the time. Don't get me wrong, I'd been ejaculating for some time. I mean, from time to time over a period of time, I don't mean like one long stream of semen all afternoon. I mean — Oh you see what I mean!! I was thirteen and I was invited to a friend's house. A girl. I'll call this girl Cathy. I remember her last name, but I'm not going to use it. I don't want to. Not that I think she's here or anything, she's probably dead by now. What a terrible thing to say. I must have a wealth of repressed hostility for this Cathy character. Anyway, I'm still not going to tell you her last name, because one of you might know her and you might tell her about this, that she's being discussed. And then, she might come

here and try to shoot me. Who knows what kind of depravity she's lapsed into in the last seven years. I have to protect myself!! I think I'll call her Mona. Oh, I already said her name was Cathy — HELL! She invited me to a party. There were lots of little boys and girls at this party. And Mona had, I assume, a crush on me. Or else, she was insane with a persecution complex and she was punishing herself by leading me to the bathroom, where she turned off the lights and "did things" to me.

And she was not a pretty girl. I realize that's sexist, but fuck it. Mona had these big, buck teeth. Now everything is relative, but these teeth were big and buck compared to just about everything else on the planet today — or then. Big teeth! Like Mr. Ed, whom at thirteen, I found amusing, but not attractive, and certainly not the object of any sexual desire. NO ALAN STRANG AM I! She turned off the lights. I was unbelievably grateful. She kissed me ... I kissed her back. We didn't actually kiss each other. It was like tennis. That's odd. But you know what I mean, don't you? I hope so. And then it happened.

I got this big hard-on. And Cathy — I mean Mona! — felt it against her leg, reached down to touch it and let out a howl like I had a hermit crab down there, that'd just ripped off her fingers! She burst out of the room, ran into the party, screaming and carrying on and telling everyone about my *"boner"* and I just wanted to die right then and there.

ESCANABA IN DA MOONLIGHT

BY JEFF DANIELS

RANGER TOM T. TREADO — early 40s.

SYNOPSIS: When the Soady clan reunites for the opening day of deer season at the family's Upper Peninsula camp, thirty-five-year-old Reuben Soady brings with him the infamous reputation of being the oldest Soady in the history of the Soadys never to bag a buck. But something mysterious is at work in these woods. Strange lights are seen and voices are heard, and soon a local forest ranger arrives with a story of a supernatural encounter. In a hunting story to beat all hunting stories, ESCANABA IN DA MOONLIGHT spins a hilarious tale of humor, horror and heart as Reuben goes to any and all lengths to remove himself from the wrong end of the family record book.

RANGER TOM.   I saw the light.
[…]
RANGER TOM.   No, the light. The light you see right before you see God. I was out combin' the area for irregularities. We've gotta lotta orange comin' up over the bridge tonight, gotta go out, show a presence. When all of a sudden, it came to me. This big, round ball of light. Right along the tree line. Lit up the whole ridge. And right in the middle of it was this, some kinda, I don't know. I couldn't tell what it was. But it held me there. I fell to my knees and started praying. Because it was God! It had to be God because suddenly words were coming out of my mouth. Words I'd never said before. Words I didn't know the meaning of. It was as if — this is gonna sound crazy, but it was as if someone else were inside my body. Speaking through me. I lost all sense of time. And

39

place. And my place in time. I began questioning my own reason for being. My mind was racing with a never-ending stream of ceaseless, incessant contemplation examining and reexamining the relevance of my sad excuse for a life, clinging to a deeply seeded faith versus modern society's insistence that if mankind cannot explain it, it can't possibly exist. Or is that —
[...]
RANGER TOM.   — simply a reflection of the world we live in. Or I live in. Or the way I choose to live in the world. And what kind of world do I live in? If I even live in a world? Is this a world? And if it is, am I in it? And if I am, why am I in it? For what purpose? There's no useful purpose to my existence. There's no method behind whatever madness was orchestrated on my behalf that spent the time, energy and spiritual wherewithal to make sure that, dammit, at least this mass of flesh, blood and bones, this polluted river of a human being, this carcass with a pulse gets to breathe the air, drink the water and eat the food of this more than likely, one and only, worldly world of worlds. *(Singing himself to sleep.)* Swing low, sweet chariot …

EVERY SEVENTEEN MINUTES THE CROWD GOES CRAZY!

BY PAUL ZINDEL

DAN — is glad the family is gone. He'll take over. A fast-food freak. He wants to be a politician or a lawyer.

SYNOPSIS: A family of exuberant and startled kids are left to fend for themselves by their mother and father — who have taken off to pursue forever a life of betting at trotter racetracks and playing black-jack in Native American casinos! An expandable chorus punctuates with hilarious and stinging sound bites this highly theatrical and poignant legend of parental abdication.

DAN. The only thing I noticed different about my mother was the way she would sit around the house crying a lot — which, I suppose, is unusual for a psychotherapist. She seemed obsessed with the case history of this one child patient she had. She kept printing out copies of it and leaving it around our breakfast table and at the neighborhood ashrams and supermarkets. It was something horrible that had happened to a ten-year-old boy at Christmas. His parents were loaded. Filthy rich. The father was a Hollywood producer. His mother was a mutual funds feminist. And they wanted to surprise their son with the greatest Christmas ever — so they bought him wonderful things: a Schwinn ten-speed; rollerblades; a Lionel electric train set, skis, a sled, a tennis racket, a dog, candy, a BB pistol, a Swiss army knife — a Christmas tree flooded with gift-wrapped boxes and bows and tinsel everywhere. A huge living room crammed with presents and

41

candy canes. They had created this dream for their son, and on Christmas morning, their son came down the stairs into the living room — this ten-year-old boy saw this fantasy they bought him — and he burst into tears! "What's the matter, son?" his father cried out, rushing to him, holding him, hugging him — "Is there something you had your heart set on that you don't see? Is there something we forgot?" And the kid, wailing through his tears, said, "I don't know, but there *could* be. There COULD be!" And that was when his father took back his hand and slapped his son with all his might. He slapped him and slapped him and slapped him!

AN EXPERIMENT WITH AN AIR PUMP

BY SHELAGH STEPHENSON

JOSEPH FENWICK — a physician and scientist.

SYNOPSIS: The play takes place in a home in Northern England in 1799 and the present day — eras on the threshold of new centuries and new worlds. In 1799 the Fenwick household awaits a future in which Dr. Fenwick believes science will bring about an enlightened democratic society. But Fenwick is blind to the ignorance and inequalities right under his nose. His protege, Armstrong, recklessly toys with the affections of Isobel, the crippled servant girl, and his daughter Maria pines after her faithless fiancé in India. Meanwhile, in the present day, all of the scientific advancements of the past 200 years have produced more questions. Ellen is a geneticist, who inherited the house from her mother. The upkeep for the old house is expensive, and she and her husband, Tom, may have to sell it. Ellen has been offered a good job, which might mean they could keep the house, but Tom has ethical problems with the job because it involves fetal tissue research. And into this mix comes the mystery of the skeleton of a long dead girl found buried under the kitchen floor.

FENWICK. *[Do,]* I do love you, but perhaps we interpret the word in different ways. You talk of tenderness when you talk of love, you talk of dogged devotion, you make it all sweet nothings and new hair ribbons —
[SUSANNAH.   I dispute the last, but for the rest, what else is love but tender devotion —]
FENWICK.   I was in thrall to you Susannah. Sick, weak with longing at the merest hint of your presence. I couldn't sleep for

43

thinking of the web of veins that traced the inside of your arms. I dreamt of the scent of your neck, the soft, suckable lobe of your ear. I wanted to crush your mouth against mine, I wanted to run my tongue down the cleft your breasts —

[SUSANNAH. *Joseph, please, this is bedroom talk* —]

FENWICK. — I wanted to lose myself inside you. Your beauty possessed me, it made my blood dance. I could watch the pulse flickering in your wrist and feel sick with desire. But because you were beautiful I imagined you to be wise, and yes I know now, as I knew then, that one has nothing to do with the other. I asked myself even then, do I love her because she is beautiful or is she beautiful because I love her. I couldn't answer and I didn't care. Passion distorts, it makes things seem what they are not. Because you had the face of the Madonna, I imbued you with her qualities. You had no conversation then, and I told myself that still waters run deep. Your looks of blank incomprehension I read as philosophical musing. When I talked of politics or science, and your face betrayed no expression whatsoever I saw it as profound spiritual calm, a stillness which put my passion to shame, I saw in you a wisdom which I could never hope to attain. The less you said the easier it was to invent you. You could have sat at my side and warbled in Japanese and I would have hung onto your every word. I dreamt of your flesh, I wanted to lick your eyes, I wanted to leave children inside you ...

EYES FOR CONSUELA

BY SAM SHEPARD

from the story "The Blue Bouquet" by Octavio Paz

HENRY — middle-aged.

SYNOPSIS: A disheveled man wakes from a nightmare, furiously shaking his clothes free of possible small jungle creatures, and dresses to face the dreamlike reality of remote Mexico. Henry is a lost soul from the American middle-class, a stranger to a wife he left hundreds of miles away in snowbound Michigan, and now alone in a squalid, vine-shrouded "hotel" amid snakes, lizards and ghosts. The owner of the inn, Viejo, warns him to stay put for his own safety, but on a brief walk he is set upon by a peasant named Amado. The predatory figure bears a machete and a slender knife which he will use to cut the eyes from Henry's head, in order to present this penitent, macabre offering of "a bouquet of blue eyes" to the bewitching Consuela. The fervor of Amado's obsessed mission, his dizzying persuasiveness, and his menacing wit and insight, push Henry's sanity to its limits. In a duel of ironic pathos, humor, cruelty and metaphor, each man examines what has taken him from the woman he loves and what desperate sacrificial price might reunite him with her. At the point when the gracefully haunting Consuela appears before Henry only to dismiss his brown eyes, the sole road out of the tangled tropical forest seems indistinct but at last possible.

HENRY. No — look — I — I am an ordinary man. Just a plain old everyday average ordinary American man. I come from an ordinary background. Generations of ordinariness. There is nothing — absolutely nothing inside me that can even begin to comprehend this stuff. I don't want to be involved in this type of thing.

I simply want to return to the *known world*. Something safe and simple. My wife. My children. My house. My car. My dog. The front lawn. My mobile phone! The Internet! Things I can put my fingers on. Tangible things in the real world! Do you understand me? I don't want to be dealing with madness now. Ghosts and sacrifices! Superstition and visions. We're approaching the millennium here! Things have moved beyond all that. Don't you have any concept at all of the outside world? The global perspective? The Bigger Picture! The *todo el mundo!* There's been an explosion of information out there! It's available to anybody now. Even people in the jungle. People like you. People completely removed from civilization. There's no secrets. There's no hocus-pocus. Everybody knows everything there is to know about absolutely everything! Electricity has delivered us! We're on the verge of breaking into territories never dreamed of before. Territories beyond the imagination. Things which will set us free so we don't have to be gouging each other's eyes out. So we don't have to be torturing and butchering each other like a bunch of diseased animals. So we don't have to be lost out here — totally lost and — wandering — without — without a clue — where we stand — in the scheme of things. Just completely — cut off.

FREEDOMLAND

BY AMY FREED

SETH — 33. A survivalist. His hard life is starting to show. Physically rugged, threatening, but with an unexpected beauty or delicacy somewhere in him. Like his sisters, blazingly sincere.

SYNOPSIS: Ages ago, Noah and his wife took their kids to the amusement park, "Freedomland." After that trip, Noah's wife ran off and left him to raise the family. Now a retired professor of religion, Noah has married Claude, a sex therapist, and lives a secluded life in the family farmhouse. Breaking this seclusion are Noah's two daughters and son who return home for an impromptu reunion. Polly, an eternally lost Greek-studies major, is the first to arrive. In pursuit is her ferocious sister, Sigrid, a painter of clowns, with a befuddled magazine interviewer in tow. Soon after, their brother Seth, a survivalist, arrives with a backwoods pregnant girlfriend. An overdue showdown between Seth and his father sets off fireworks that illuminate the neurosis, rage and anxiety of one family — and of America at the turn of the millennium.

SETH. *(Enters with venison haunches, wrapped and tied in a bloody package. His speech is offhandedly punctuated by the actions that illustrate his butchering skills.)* These deer come down right into our backyard. I've put in a lot of vegetables and they love to raid the garden. It's become a real problem keeping them out. But we've got meat now. So we freeze it, we salt it and we dry it. It's not such a big deal when you remember. Boys Chase Squirrels Climbing High. Bleed Cool Skin Clean Hang. First thing after the kill — *(Swings deer onto table.)* — You have to behead it or cut the jugular vein. Lori puts a bowl underneath, and we like to save the blood for sausage. I had to gut this carcass in a hurry, because I hit her in the liver first, and a ruptured organ can be bad news.

(Slashes at the wrapping and demonstrating matter-of-factly.) What I do is, I cut off the feet, and turn her on her back. Slit the skin at the breastbone. Insert your free hand, like this, and press the inner organs down as you continue to cut, all the way to the asshole. Now, if it had been a buck I would have cut off its dick and balls. The biggest nuisance is they carry so many fleas and ticks. *(Looks up.)* I thought maybe we all could have some for dinner. Freeze the rest.

GINT

BY ROMULUS LINNEY

from Henrik Ibsen's *Peer Gynt*

OLDER MAN — an explosive mountain preacher.

SYNOPSIS: Pete Gint is a ragged young man in the Appalachian Mountains in 1917 who spends most of his time lying, drinking and getting into trouble. Gint is determined to become "something great grand and glorious," but he's not sure just what that is. The first act follows Gint's sexual misadventures with a married woman and a woman who turns out to be a razorback hog, but Gint's true love is Sally Vicks. At first Sally disdains Gint, but slowly he wins her over. As they move into a humble mountain cabin, however, the hog woman shows up with Gint's bastard son. Not wanting Sally to be hurt or disgraced by "this nastiness," Gint leaves Appalachia and travels far away. Years pass, and now Gint is 75 and a billionaire. He calls together several other powerful billionaires for he has a dream of founding a new country, based solely on corporations. The billionaires have other plans. They have secretly taken over Gint's companies and he is cast out and back into the wilderness. Gint then begins a nightmarish journey home, encountering a mountain funeral, a Cherokee medicine man, and battling lunatics and devils until he arrives back in the arms of Sally Vicks.

OLDER MAN
He come to Cave Cove at war time
our soldiers went proudly to death World War I
him standing before the army
showing sergeants a right arm one hand gone
him two handed
three days before

he never denied what he done
[...]
He went to live hard above the waterfalls
found a wife who took him
children soon
and to them he was not a disgrace
coming to town with that stump arm
getting his week's supply of our scorn
along with his bread
(He gets evangelistic and emotional.)
flood washed him out
never a word of complaint
fire burned down his cabin
he rebuilt that
with that stump arm
and prospered again
the worst winter we ever knowed
blasted his crops killed his wife nearly
finished him but onct again
the tiny farm gave forth its life
to a one-handed draft dodger
(He quiets down.)
then his children grown up and handsome
went off and forgot him
having learned
to be ashamed of their father
and he lived alone with his disgrace
through other days
and other wars
(Emotional again.)
Oh my God
modern wars
men come back crazy from that war
they took drugs to ease
memories of women and children slaughtered
what they had done to others
and suffered themselves for their country
and still can't forget

while he who cut off his hand
farmed forgotten
until this morning when he died
[...]
(Quiets down again.)
So we have come together to bury this man
he was no neighbor
he was no patriot
he grew nothing for state or church
but there on land almost upside down
he made up his mind who he was
he saw his humble calling in his life
and there he quietly lived
because he was himself
because he paid his price openly before us
his silence in war rang true
(He suddenly preaches hellfire.)
before he'd kill a man with that right hand
he cut it off
like the Bible says
if thy right hand offend thee
like the Bible says
cut it off and he did it
he didn't just say it
oh no my God he did it
praise God
[...]
Therefore whatever we may think
of his duty in that time of war
let peace be with him now
it is not for us to judge the heart
or the dust to which it falls
that is for heaven
but let me dare to speak for him here
I hope this man self crippled in our life
stands whole and true before God
Amen

GIVE ME YOUR ANSWER, DO!

BY BRIAN FRIEL

TOM CONNOLLY — He is in his middle-to-late 50s. His dress is casual-to-shabby.

SYNOPSIS: The play is set in the home of the impoverished Irish novelist, Tom Connolly, and his wife, Daisy, whose lives are overshadowed by their permanently hospitalized daughter. They are visited by Daisy's parents and by the successful novelist, Garret Fitzgerald, and his wife, Gráinne. The question at the heart of the play is: Will Connolly sell his manuscripts to a Texas university (as Fitzgerald has just done) and thus acquire some much-needed money? This is a story of people inextricably bound together and of the loves and hates that that proximity generates.

TOM. My new novel? Yes, yes, yes, I was waiting for that question. We've had a surfeit of your cheeky jokes on that subject over the years, haven't we?

Well, I'll tell you about it. Took it out again yesterday morning. Went back over all the notes. Looked at all the bits I'd written and tossed aside over the past five years. Read very carefully the twenty-three pages I'd already written. And I can tell you, madam, let me tell you there just may be something there. I don't want to say anymore at this stage. But I did get a little — a little quiver — a whiff — a stirring of a sense that perhaps — maybe —

But that's all I'm going to say at this point. I dare not say anymore. But if it were to emerge for me, my darling; if I could coax it out; if I could hold it and then release it into its contented rest, into its happy completion, then, my silent love, my strange little offspring, then I would come straight back here to you and fold you in my arms; and you and I would climb into a golden balloon — just the two of us — only the two of us — and we would soar above this earth and float away forever across the face of the "darkly, deeply, beautifully blue sky."

THE HOLOGRAM THEORY

BY JESSICA GOLDBERG

SIMON SPENCE — 40s, Julian's father, a successful film director.

SYNOPSIS: A beautiful, young Trinidadian artist, Patsy, is awakened one night to a vision of her twin brother, Dominic, whom she hasn't seen in five years. Unbeknownst to Patsy, he has been murdered, and his restless ghost summons her to unravel the mystery of his death and what was once his life. Patsy travels to the decadent, seductive and terrifying underworld of New York City and finds herself in a foreign world — a vast landscape of club kids, like Julian and Mimi, cops and jaded journalists. As she learns more about the brutal world her brother once inhabited, as well his own brutality, Patsy struggles with complex feelings about her past, familial obligations and the spirit world.

SIMON. I look at you and I try to understand, I try. I try to see it in you, how you got this way, this, this. We tried to help you, we got you help. You've robbed me, you've robbed your mother. I can't, I can't, and yet I can somehow, but it doesn't belong to me, this, this person you've become —
[JULIAN. I changed —]
SIMON. It doesn't matter, it's already done, happened, when? Sometime outside of the baby pictures of you I have, the lessons I tried to teach you. I look at my new children, and I wonder, could this happen to them too? Is it out of your hands? Do you lose it all somewhere along the way? This child you stare at in the crib, does it disappear, and you recognize nothing?
[JULIAN. The sixth at ten A.M., I won't forget.]
SIMON. I just don't know. I just don't know.

IMPOSSIBLE MARRIAGE

BY BETH HENLEY

SYDNEY LUNT — 20s, with a beard and wire glasses.

SYNOPSIS: The entire action of the play takes place in Kandall Kingsley's beautiful and mysterious garden. Kandall's youngest daughter, Pandora, is to be wed to Edvard Lunt, a worldly artist twice her age. Kandall does not think the match to be at all suitable. Floral, Pandora's older sister, who is expecting a child at any moment, plots to break off the marriage. Unexpectedly, Sidney Lunt, the groom's son, arrives with a note from his mother in which she vows to throw herself from an attic window if the marriage goes forward. Even Reverend Lawrence who has come to wed the couple has secret hopes and desperate desires.

SIDNEY. Marriage is an evilly antiquated institution. A suffocating environment where banality is bred.
[...]
SIDNEY. [...] Love has yet to avail itself to my scrutiny.
[...]
SIDNEY. [...] There was this one girl I liked. We would chat and talk about ice cream selection. She worked behind the counter and offered me unlimited free samples in small midget spoons. Often I couldn't make a decision, or up my mind, and would ask for her recommendation. Her preference. I would put it to her like this, "Which flavor would you get?" I always enjoyed whatever she selected or chose, until one day she picked Pistachio. I wasn't pleased with it. It wasn't up my alley. I told her this and she gave me a new cone. The Rocky Road. She took the Pistachio from me, threw it in a canister, and said I was not to pay her for it. I knew she couldn't be giving out free cones. I was aware the price of the second cone would be deducted from her small wages. So I left

money for it. The cone. Too much money really, but I could not stand to wait for change. I never came back, of course, because it may have been an uncomfortable situation. Anyway, it could never have been the same.

IN THE BLOOD

BY SUZAN-LORI PARKS

DOCTOR — Hester's doctor.

SYNOPSIS: In this modern day riff on The Scarlet Letter, *Hester La Negrita, a homeless mother of five, lives with her kids on the tough streets of the inner city. Her eldest child is teaching her how to read and write, but the letter "A" is, so far, the only letter she knows. Her five kids are named Jabber, Bully, Trouble, Beauty and Baby, and the characters are played by adult actors who double as five other people in Hester's life: her ex-boyfriend, her social worker, her doctor, her best friend and her minister. While Hester's kids fill her life with joy — lovingly comical moments amid the harsh world of poverty — the adults with whom she comes in contact only hold her back. Nothing can stop the play's tragic end.*

DOCTOR.
Times are tough:
What can we do?
When I see a woman begging on the streets I guess I could
Bring her in my house
sit her at my table
make her a member of my family, sure.
But there are hundreds and thousands of them
and my house cant hold them all.
Maybe we should all take in just one.
Except they wouldnt really fit.
They wouldnt really fit in with us.
Theres such a gulf between us. What can we do?
I am a man of the people from way back my streetside practice is
a testament to that

57

so dont get me wrong
do not for a moment think that I am one of those people haters
    who does not understand who does not experience — compassion.
(Rest.)
Shes been one of my neediest cases for several years now.
What can I do?
Each time she comes to me
looking more and more forlorn
and more and more in need
of affection.
At first I wouldnt touch her without gloves on, but then
(Rest.)
We did it once
in that alley there
she was
phenomenal.
(Rest.)
I was
lonesome and
She gave herself to me in a way that I had never experienced
even with women Ive paid
she was, like she was giving me something that was not hers to give
    me but something that was mine
that Id lent her
and she was returning it to me.
Sucked me off for what seemed like hours
but I was very insistent. And held back
and she understood that I wanted her in the traditional way.
And she was very giving very motherly very obliging very
    understanding
very phenomenal.
Let me cumm inside her. Like I needed to.
What could I do?
I couldnt help it.

THE JOY OF GOING SOMEWHERE DEFINITE

BY QUINCY LONG

RAYMOND — a middle-aged logger, and a passionate, mercurial, comic leader.

SYNOPSIS: Three out-of-work loggers, fueled by alcohol, God and song, set forth from a northwoods bar one night on a misguided errand of mercy. Raymond, Merle and Junior have met a stranger in the bar even drunker and lonelier than they are, and, after accidentally shooting him, decide to reunite the poor fellow with his estranged wife somewhere north of the border in Canada. Hampered at every turn by misunderstanding, confusion, stupidity, drunkenness, desire and mistaken identity, the chivalrous loggers resolutely attempt to do the right thing, while achieving precisely the opposite. In the end, wild certainty yields to a chastened amazement over what man won't do for a little peace.

RAYMOND.
    Don't you think I know it
    How you think I like it Junior
    Cuttin' myself shaving all alone
    Oh I could take and be my own woman sure
    Put on the bra and panties and pretend
    Parade around in my room to the radio
    But I don't do that
    Won't do that
    Just like I won't go with Patsy
    Just isn't in my makeup
    Don't you see
    It's plain as your nose Junior

Got nothin' to do with my wife
Or I don't have a wife
It's your wife
His wife
Anybody's wife
Mankind's wife that's at stake here
And you can buy her a gown
Wrap her in love
Mount her on a bearskin
But in the end don't matter what you do
They wanta get out they're gonna go
Gonna run like a cheap T-shirt
Open their faucets and run wild
You can't hold 'em from it
And you can't make 'em love you when they don't
But you sure as hell can punish 'em

LABOR DAY

BY A.R. GURNEY

JOHN — a playwright, older man.

SYNOPSIS: John is an established older playwright recovering from a bout with cancer. His latest work, which he views as his best, if possibly his last, has gained the interest of a major regional theatre, the Shubert Organization, and a possible Hollywood star. Dennis, the bright young director to whom John has given the play, shows up on the Labor Day holiday at the writer's house in rural Connecticut to ask for essential changes. Dennis feels the play has been adversely affected by the playwright's illness, becoming too inverted and sentimental. John's family has gathered for the holiday, and when they find out the play is primarily about them, they also criticize the enterprise. It is soon obvious that the playwright — and aging father — doesn't really know either his family or himself.

JOHN. But first I want to make a little speech.
[DENNIS. Go ahead.]
JOHN. Just a short one, I promise. I want to tell you where we are, Dennis. We are living in Rome during the third century A.D. And at this point in history, the empire is seething with unruly citizens, all smoldering with resentment at the unconscionable gap between them and the ruling class. To distract them from violent revolution, we build huge amphitheaters and coliseums where brutal gladiatorial combats and elaborate theatrical spectacles satisfy their lust for blood and show. Meanwhile, an expensive, over-equipped army patrols our far-flung borders, while an ineffectual senate idly contests the non-decisions of second-rate emperors, and deplores the fact that the traditional religion is giving way to strange self-indulgent cults — like Christianity.

[DENNIS. I'm with you, John.]
JOHN. And in the midst of all this turbulence, how should the wise patrician live his life? By creating his own small circle of civility. He retreats to his farm, embraces his family and writes the occasional play.
[DENNIS. Several occasional plays.]
JOHN. All right. A number of plays designed to be performed off-Broadway, in regional theatres and in high-school auditoriums.
[DENNIS. And also overseas …]
JOHN. OK, and overseas. And which, in their brief two-hours traffic on the stage, try to create their own small circles of civility by reminding like-minded citizens of the human dimension in us all.
[DENNIS. Wow, John.]
JOHN. But circles of civility cost money, Dennis. You and my children are going to need plenty of it as the empire decays. So let's rewrite my play for Robert Redford.
[DENNIS. The speech is over?]
JOHN. The speech is over.

THE LARAMIE PROJECT

BY MOISÉS KAUFMAN AND THE
MEMBERS OF THE TECTONIC THEATER PROJECT

AARON KREIFELS — university student. 19 years old.

SYNOPSIS: In October 1998 a twenty-one-year-old student at the University of Wyoming was severely beaten and left to die, tied to a fence in the middle of the prairie outside Laramie. His bloody, bruised and battered body was not discovered until the next day, and he died in an area hospital several days later. His name was Matthew Shepard, and he was the victim of this assault because he was gay. Moisés Kaufman and members of the Tectonic Theater Project made six trips to Laramie over a year and a half in the aftermath of the beating and during the trial. They conducted over 200 interviews with people from the town and constructed a theatrical collage, exploring the depths to which humanity can sink and the heights of compassion we are also capable of.

AARON KREIFELS. Well I uh, I took off on my bicycle about five o'clock P.M. on Wednesday from my dorm. I just kinda felt like going for a ride. So I — I went up to the top of Cactus Canyon, and I'm not super familiar with that area, so on my way back down, I didn't know where I was going, I was just sort of picking the way to go, which now ... it just makes me think that God wanted me to find him because there's no way that I was going to go that way.
So I was in some deep-ass sand, and I wanted to turn around — but for some reason, I kept going. And, uh, I went along, and there was this rock, on the — on the ground — and I just drilled it. I went — over the handlebars and ended up on the ground.
So, uh, I got up, and I was just kind of dusting myself off, and

I was looking around and I noticed something — which ended up to be Matt, and he was just lying there by a fence, and I — I just thought it was a scarecrow. I was like, Halloween's coming up, thought it was a Halloween gag, so I didn't think much of it, so I got my bike, walked it around the fence that was there. And uh, got closer to him and I noticed his hair — and that was a major key to me, noticing it was a human being — was his hair. 'Cause I just thought it was a dummy, seriously, I noticed — I even noticed the chest going up and down, I still thought it was a dummy, you know. I thought it was just like some kind of mechanism.

But when I saw hair, well I knew it was a human being.

So ... I ran to the nearest house and — I just ran as fast as I could ... and called the police.

LAST TRAIN TO NIBROC

BY ARLENE HUTTON

RALEIGH — 21 or 22. From a small town in Kentucky. Just a good guy, slow to anger and quick to chuckle.

SYNOPSIS: In December 1940, an east-bound cross-country train carries the bodies of the great American writers Nathanael West and F. Scott Fitzgerald. Also on board is May, who shares her seat with a charming young flyer, Raleigh. Religious and bookish, May plans to be a missionary. Raleigh has been given a medical discharge and is heading to New York to be a writer. Raleigh and May discover they are from neighboring Appalachian towns, and he decides to change trains for Kentucky, promising to take May to the next Nibroc Festival. Scene Two finds May and Raleigh at the festival, but a year and half later. Unfit for war, and needing to support his parents, Raleigh has been working in a Detroit factory. May is teaching school and dating an itinerant preacher. When Raleigh confronts her, May admits her prejudices against his family. It is not until the following spring as they sit on May's front porch, watching a lumberyard fire in the distance, that the two are finally able to resolve their differences and discover the depth of their feelings. May accepts Raleigh's sudden proposal to elope, as the sky grows red like a sunrise.

RALEIGH. Well, now. You're going home. See, you should be happy. Another few hours and you can change trains for Kentucky.
[MAY. You, too.]
RALEIGH. *[Nope.]* I'm staying. On the train. Going to New York City. Funny, when I got on, boarded the train, back in Los Angelees, I was going home. Not happy about it, but going home. I got on this train. Thought, I can go anywhere. Chicago, any-

where. No one's expecting me. No one knows I'm coming. Got a uniform still on, got a pass. Anywhere I want to go.

[...]

RALEIGH. I can go anywhere. Thought about Detroit, lots of work in the factories there, my brother-in-law says, but I can go do that any time.

[MAY. You don't want to go home?]

RALEIGH. *[Nope.]* Home'll always be there. I got on this train, and the conductor told me that the coffins were being loaded in. That Nathanael West and F. Scott Fitzgerald were riding the same train I was. So, don't you see, I can't let that go by. When would something like that ever happen again?

[MAY. You didn't know them.]

RALEIGH. *[I didn't know you, either, but now]* we're riding the same train. And no matter what happens, there will always have been a time that we rode the train together. Things are affected by other things. And I can't let that go by. That I'm on the train with the two greatest writers of this century. And I thought I've just got to stay on this train. Follow those men. This is my chance, my time, and if I don't take it now, don't move right now, not later, now, while I'm supposed to, it'll never happen again.

LOVE AND UNDERSTANDING

BY JOE PENHALL

NEAL — a young man.

SYNOPSIS: Live-in lovers Neal and Rachel are overworked doctors. They rarely see each other and their relationship suffers for it. Enter Neal's old good-for-nothing friend, Richie, for a surprise visit. He needs a place to stay and Neal is too weak to say no. Rachel doesn't want him either, but Richie manipulates her, creating a sexual tension between them. Richie immediately uses this charge to stir up trouble between the couple, insinuating that Neal is boring and that Rachel needs a good time with a black sheep like himself. And while he works on Rachel, Richie steals drugs from Neal's office. Rachel tells Neal about the pass, but Richie denies it. Thinking Neal doesn't care, Rachel sleeps with Richie, but the couple is caught by Neal. Richie almost delights in the trouble he's caused, and with more drugs, ends up comatose from an overdose. The strain of all that's happened causes Rachel and Neal to split up. Richie recovers and takes off for Wales, leaving Neal and Rachel with a newfound understanding of one another which may or may not lead to reconciliation.

NEAL.   I wanted you, I just wanted … you. *(Pause. He drinks.)* I had a dream about you last night. We were on a roof and it was very dark, nighttime, brilliant stars in the sky. It was a roof party. A barbecue on a midsummer night. And you could see right across London, all the places we'd lived together. The river and the embankment and the water glittering in the dark. And I wasn't really talking to you but you came over in a black dress and started talking to me. You were laughing insistently at something or other

67

and I started laughing, humouring you, in my dream, and then I saw it. This thing on your breast, like a broach, over your heart. A cluster. As I got closer I saw it was a nest of maggots. And as we were laughing the maggots grew and hatched more maggots. And I thought of Richie. And that's when I finally knew it was over. I would never be in love with you again. We'd walk away from each other quite calmly and you'd never even notice you had this thing clinging to you. Nobody would. Only I would. *(Pause.)* And then I realised it wasn't maggots at all. It was rice pudding. Or bubble and squeak. That's what you'd been laughing about. Bubble and squeak all down your dress. And I went to kiss you. And I woke up. *(Pause.)* What do you think it means.

MARCUS IS WALKING

BY JOAN ACKERMANN

HENRY — a young man.

SYNOPSIS: Eleven vignettes in an automobile examine the emotional landscape we roam as we travel in our cars. Control, navigation, love and escape are some of the themes explored. A protective father shepherds his son through the neighborhood on Halloween; an actor on his way to perform Hamlet provokes a rear-end collision and confrontation with a Czech émigré cab driver; a devastated businessman strikes up an unlikely alliance with a homeless woman who sleeps in his car. This is the landscape of human frailty and vulnerability, charm and strength; a playwright's whimsy combined with a shrewd sense of observation.

HENRY. *(Simply.)* Lisa, I love you.
[LISA. Henry ...
HENRY. I do.
LISA. You don't have to say that.]
HENRY. *[But]* I do. Love you. For me not to say it, not to acknowledge it, would be like not acknowledging a little rain cloud inside the car, pouring rain. There *isn't* one, but if there *were* one, it would be very odd not to comment on it. Actually, it feels kind of like a storm, in my system, these emotions, that I have for you. They're terribly distracting, I can't focus properly, can't do *anything* really without this constant disturbance, like a swarm of bees inside and outside me ... this tumultuous ... uh ... *obsession* with you. It's hard to describe. Sometimes, when I'm with you, Lisa, I feel like there are three people in the room: you, me and this ... tangle of emotions zooming around, wild patterns, protons, neutrons, racing, this sculpture that I happen to be carrying around inside me.

You know I'm normally pretty witty, my friends think I'm *funny*, but when I'm with you my, I just, my tongue gets shipwrecked on my teeth. I have to say that it's not entirely *pleasant* being so completely uncontrollably smitten by you. There's actually quite a bit of pain involved that ... a *lot* of pain I can't do much about, but ... Lisa, you touch something so deep in me ... I felt it the instant I met you, I had to run out of the room. Your voice, your language, these phrases you come up with — "loaded for bear," "boardinghouse reach" when you reached across me in the conference room for pizza, "boardinghouse reach" I love that, I just ... how you talk, your eyes, your handwriting. Physically, I find you incredibly sexy but that's the least of it ... I love watching you watch things, I do, I could watch you watching things forever ... your sense of ... I'm babbling I know not very likely making much but ... if I can just at least try to express ... No one has ever made me feel the way that you do. I know, I realize it's *my* problem, I'm not dumping all this on you, I'm the one who has to deal with it, but I *am* in love with you. *(Pause.)* I guess we should go.

MERCY

BY LAURA CAHILL

STU — 20s/30s.

SYNOPSIS: On Manhattan's Upper West Side, Sarah decides to brighten her spirits, and those of her friend Isobel, by throwing an impromptu dinner party. Sarah invites Bo, a wanna-be singer who, to the dismay of Isobel, invites Stu, Isobel's ex-boyfriend. Isobel is deeply depressed over the break-up. She can barely look at Stu when he arrives; but, fighting through tears, she seeks only understanding and compassion from him. Feeling betrayed, Isobel has no other option but to wrestle her demons while feigning cordiality and contentment in the face of Sarah and Bo. Soon, the dinner party develops into an awkward facade of lost souls whose failure to communicate and find happiness has left them pitiful, hopelessly lonely and at the mercy of others.

STU. I've already written one novel.
[…]
STU. Yeah. I submitted it to Random House.
[…]
STU. Well, I knew this guy who I went all the way through school with in Pennsylvania. He was a real dork actually, I mean you never would in a million years expect this guy to have even made anything of himself, you know, he just didn't "have" it. I don't know how the hell he became so important, but he's an editor anyway at Random House. So I called him up and he was like "Oh great," and we had lunch and he invited me and a bunch of the other guys from our group in high school to a big party once and I saw Jay McInerney there. So, um, anyway, I told him I'm writing this novel and he said, "Oh, sure, just send it to me," and so I did and yesterday I got a letter back. And it was from an assistant.

That asshole didn't even give me enough respect to take my manuscript and put it on the top of his own desk and read it and then let me know what he thought. I don't know who the Bozo is who read it or how qualified they even were to give me their opinion. *[ISOBEL. That's terrible.]*
STU. Well whatever, it doesn't really matter. I'm trying short stories now. I'm interested in the form. It challenges me. *(There's no response.)* So I'm working towards pursuing it full time.

MOJO

BY JEZ BUTTERWORTH

BABY — 20s.

SYNOPSIS: Silver Johnny is the new singing sensation, straight out of a low-life Soho clubland bar in 1958 England. His success could be the big break for two dead-end workers in the bar, if they play their cards right and trust the owner of the place to make a good deal with the local money mogul. Before they can dream what to do with all the money they'll make, the owner turns up dead, Silver Johnny disappears, the second in command takes over the bar and power positions are juggled about. Going through the uppers and downers filched from pocketbooks, and trying to keep a lid on the precocious anger of the dead owner's son, the band of losers figures out the law of the streets and who killed the boss, but not in time to save one of their own, and perhaps their souls.

BABY. ... I was about nine, bit younger, and my dad tells me we're driving to the country for the day.

He's got this half-share in this caff at the time, and it was doing really badly, so he was always really busy working day and night, so like, this was totally out of the blue.

So I got in his van with him, and we drive off and I notice that in the front of the cab there's this bag of sharp knives. And like a saw and a big meat cleaver.

And I thought, "This is it. He's going to kill me. He's going to take me off and kill me once and for all." And I sat there in silence all the way to Wales and I knew that day I was about to die.

So we drive till it goes dark, and Dad pulls the van into this field. And he switches off the lights. And we sit there in silence. And there's all these cows in the field, watching us. And suddenly

73

Dad slams his foot down and we ram this fucking great cow clean over the top of the van. And it tears off the bonnet and makes a great dent in the top, but it was dead all right. See we'd gone all the way to Wales to rustle us a cow. For the caff.

Now a dead cow weighs half a ton. So you've got to cut it up there and then. And I was so relieved I had tears in my eyes. And we hacked that cow to pieces, sawing, chopping, ripping, with all the other cows standing around in the dark, watching.

Then when we'd finished, we got back in the cab and drove back to town. Covered in blood.

THE MOST FABULOUS STORY EVER TOLD

BY PAUL RUDNICK

TREY — an acerbic, very gay man dressed as Santa Claus.

SYNOPSIS: A stage manager, headset and prompt book at hand, brings the house lights out and cues the creation of the world. Act One recounts the major episodes of the Old Testament, with a twist: instead of Adam and Eve, our lead characters are Adam and Steve, and Jane and Mabel, a lesbian couple with whom they decide to start civilization. Along the way, Mabel and Adam invent God, but Jane and Steve are skeptical. This brings about the Flood, during which Steve has an affair with a rhinoceros and invents infidelity. No longer blissful, Adam and Steve break up only to be reunited as two of the wise men at the Nativity. Act Two jumps to modern day Manhattan. Adam and Steve are together again, and Steve is HIV-positive. It's Christmas Eve, and Jane is nine months pregnant. The two women want to marry and want Adam and Steve to join them in the ceremony. A wheelchair-bound, Jewish lesbian rabbi arrives to officiate. The ceremony is interrupted as Jane gives birth, and Steve confides to Adam that his medication isn't working and that he'll probably not survive much longer. Bound by their long life together, and the miracle of birth they've just witnessed, the two men comfort each other even though they know their remaining time together will be short.

TREY. I am an over-bred, over-educated WASP from Connecticut, so I've always thought of God as, you know — an ancestor. But lately Adam's been going on, about miracles, and his little Bible pageant, so I thought, well, I'll try. *(Noticing Cheryl's poinsettia plant.)* Oh look, it's a poinsettia — the gift that won't die. So I don ensemble and I volunteer, on Christmas Eve, at the local homeless shelter. Where I have just allowed countless heartbreakingly innocent, bright-eyed homeless children to sit on my lap. "Ho, ho, ho, and what would you like for Christmas, little Simbali, or Jamal, or Tylenol?" I can make these jokes because my name is Trey, and my brothers are named Shreve and Stone, so who am I to talk? And little Advil says, "Santa, whassup? Is you a faggot?"

[...]

TREY. Well, I took a deep breath, and I said, "Why yes I am, little Midol. And the North Pole is for everyone, gay and straight."

[...]

TREY. Armageddon. The child's hardworking, down-on-her-luck single parent grabs the child off my lap and screams, "Get away, cocksucker!" To which I reply, "But darling, look what I've brought for you — Christmas crack." And finally the director of the shelter says that maybe it's best if *I* leave! So I come here, and my question for you, Adam, is this — what the fuck is God thinking?

MY BOY JACK

BY DAVID HAIG

GUARDSMAN BOWE — late teens, 20s, member of Jack's platoon of Irish Guards.

SYNOPSIS: The year is 1913. War with Germany is imminent. Rudyard Kipling, the British Empire's greatest apologist, is at the peak of his literary fame. This play explores the nature of a man who loses his balance when devotion to family and country clash. World War I breaks out, and Kipling's son, Jack, is determined to fight, but the Army and the Navy both reject him because of his extremely poor eyesight. Undaunted, Kipling uses his influence to land Jack a commission in the Irish Guards, sparking off a bitter family conflict. Jack goes to war and is reported missing, believed wounded, in his first action. The Kipling family live in vain hope for two years, before finally learning of Jack's death. The effect on Kipling is profound and irrevocable, as he struggles to confront his appalling sense of guilt and loss.

BOWE.   The waitin' to go over's the worst ... You want to talk to your man next to yous, but you can't. The skin on your face is stretched so tight, you feel if you speak, it'd split and peel away ... you're on your own ... completely ... d'you know what I see when I do go over the top?
[RUDYARD.   What?]
BOWE.   A game of football! A bunch of arseholes dribblin' a football across no man's land ... the next regiment's attackin' the Boche — with their rifles shouldered, kickin' a football ... in midair the ball disappears, and they start fallin' over — all of 'em ... there's a bloke stridin' out with a walkin' stick, like a gent on a Sunday jaunt in Phoenix Park. He disappears into the smoke ... then the machine guns ... the Maxims ... I dump the shovel, I've

got no choice. The bullets are all around me — Bees! Bees! — a swarm of angry bees. Buzzin' an' racin' past the ear. Jimmy Doyle shoutin' at me: "We're the only two left Michael." ... he's hit! He goes down ... I'm runnin' and my lungs are burstin'. The din is diabolic, so loud you can't hear it, you can only feel it, feel the whole planet tremblin'. But I make it ... I fall into Jerry's front line trench ... I'm lyin' on top o' somethin', lyin' there tryin' to breathe, lyin' on top of a dead man ... practically kissin' him I'm so close to him. My uniform is soakin' wet, I look down an' the front of him is gone, an' all his insides are spillin' over the edge of him ... covered in his blood, German blood. Then ... Jesus ... I see the gas creepin' towards me, like somethin' livin' an' I know I've lost my mask. Help me Jesus, where's me fuckin' mask? ... the gas is 'round me, creepin' up me. Where's me fuckin' mask! Where's me mask! I'm breathin' it, I'm goin' to die, I'm dyin'. But the German's mask is in his hand, Mother o' God thank you, I pull it away from him, holdin' it against my face, breathin' the clean air, Jesus, I'm goin' to live. An' this Hun is after savin' my life ... someone is beside me, givin' me the thumbs-up in front of my face. I stick my thumb in the air, he's pointin' down the trench. There's more lads down there and an officer ... makin' our way down the trench ... there's a body ... Jesus this is what it's like, there's a body standin' there, standin' casual like, but he's got no head ... this is what it's like ... water ... Jesus, my lips ... water ...

NEW YORK ACTOR

BY JOHN GUARE

CRAIG — an actor.

SYNOPSIS: Several actors are sitting in a theater bar, reveling in success and failure — their own and that of their friends around them. Craig is back in New York after several seasons in Hollywood in a sitcom. So happy to be cast in an upcoming Broadway production, he doesn't mind revealing that Hollywood was not what he liked. The other stage actors agree, but would have loved the chance to do TV. There is an element of fear — that it all could disappear in a moment — along with the humor of what their lives have been like and the uncertainty of the profession. When one more actor joins them, and tells them of a part he just got, they all realize Craig's been fired and this guy is taking the role. Instead of rallying around, everyone goes their own way, leaving Craig with his greatest fear of being a has-been.

CRAIG. *[But]* I'm thrilled to be back in New York. Out there I was ready to kill myself. That's what scared me. I finally got the courage to do it.
[NAT. Kill yourself?]
CRAIG. Terminal likeability. The L.A. disease. Any time you read a freeway fatality, know it's an L.A. actor who crashed his Volvo into an overpass, sick of being likable. That's — that's what happened to me.
[EILEEN. No!]
CRAIG. I tried to crash my new Volvo into a rail guard on the freeway. I pulled over to the side of the road —
[NAT. Where?]
CRAIG. Out by Valencia. Asthmatic. Gasping for breath. Sweating. Freezing. My series was canceled. Going through yet

79

another pilot season. No pilot. My daughter comes to me and says, "Daddy, I want breast implants." I said, "Francesca, you're six years old." This L.A. child looks up at me and says, "I don't give a shit. I want them and I want them now." What kind of values are these? My boy Milo is always in his mother's sewing kit. Playing with needles. We can't tell if he's going to be a junkie or a costume designer. What strangers am I raising? Katinka and I gave 'Cesca a gift certificate for some work on her nose which shut her up but only for a while and now she's here getting her head on — I hope. Katinka and I are frightened. Where was I headed? *Lawyer* canceled. I went up for another series. This time the friend of the best friend. The beginning of the downward spiral. I aimed my Volvo right into that rail guard.
[NAT. Hey, you're safe. You're here.]
CRAIG. And then the call came.
[...]
CRAIG. The difference between being an L.A. actor and a New York actor is in L.A. you don't ever dare be tuned out of somebody's living room. Never be unpleasant or complicated. But a New York actor is fearsome. A New York actor changes his soul. A New York actor has a soul to change. Christ, listen to me. I'm alive! Being what God meant me to be!

THE OLD SETTLER

BY JOHN HENRY REDWOOD

HUSBAND WITHERSPOON — black man, 29 years old. Elizabeth's roomer.

SYNOPSIS: In World War II Harlem, New York, a fifty-five-year-old spinster (or as they were called in those days — an "Old Settler") Elizabeth Borny, takes in a young male roomer, Husband Witherspoon, to help her with the rent. Husband has come to Harlem from South Carolina to search for his girlfriend, Lou Bessie Preston. Also living with Elizabeth is her sister, Quilly McGrath, fifty-three. There is an ominous cloud of tension that hangs over Elizabeth and Quilly's relationship. This tension is further exacerbated when Elizabeth and Husband take to liking each other. Quilly, who doesn't like Husband living with them in the first place, surely doesn't approve of their "carrying on," especially since Elizabeth is old enough to be Husband's mother. It is this "carrying on" that exposes a thirty-year-old wound which, until now, only had a bandage — now the wound can heal for the sisters.

HUSBAND. I did. But my mama used to say, "there's more to life than a good time." I've been up here for almost four days looking for Lou Bessie and I've seen a lot. I don't think we were meant to live on top of one another like people do up here. When I woke up in the mornings, these past few days, I used to feel low and I couldn't figure out why. Then when I got on my knees this morning to say my prayers, I tried to look up to heaven, and that's when it came to me. There ain't no windows in that room! Now, I don't mean to be talking bad about your house, Miss Elizabeth. You keep a nice, clean, comfortable house just like my mama used to. But, I can't open my eyes and see the light of day ... see the sky.

When you do look out of a window, you look into a wall or into somebody else's window. I don't hear no birds or crickets ... don't see a tree or lightning bugs. There's no place to take off your shoes and feel the grass and dirt on your bare feet. No, Miss Elizabeth, just as soon as Lou Bessie and me get things straightened out, we're going back down home just like I planned.

OUR LADY OF SLIGO

BY SEBASTIAN BARRY

DADA — presence of Mai's dead father.

SYNOPSIS: From her hospital bed in 1950s Dublin, Mai O'Hara recalls her life through morphine-induced memories and hallucinations. Dying of liver cancer caused by alcoholism, Mai reminisces on her youthful promise as a member of the Galway bourgeoisie; the death of one of her children; and of the marriage fueled by liquor, bickering and remorse, to her husband Jack, who visits her on occasion — as does the spirt of her dead father, Dada. Jack's visits to her bedside are a testament to the mutual hatred they share and the mutual dependence they have on each other. Through it all, Mai uses her mordant wit and vanity to pull her out of painful realizations. Once the first woman in Sligo to wear trousers, it emerges that Mai is not only the victim of a broken marriage, but a victim of an Ireland in which the Catholic middle-class has been nullified by spiritual and political isolation after the Civil War.

DADA.   They used to come in from the moonlight, beckoned by the candle on my table, little silver fellows from the trees, they used to come in and sit with me, I used to think, as I lingered there, reading a book of my father's, that drank the three farms. And I used to sit there and you would be there too, Mai, in the cradle in the shadow of the room. Oh, no one knows the sorrow that I felt when my father drank the three farms. For I never said a word to anyone. I pulled up my socks and tightened my belt and went to work with a will, scrivening for Burke the Insurance Agent. I was fourteen. Gone were the lambs and the fretting pony. The old scrivener in the place was a ruffian from Ballina and he spat on the back of my coat and called me a fool and the son of a failure. With my eyes fast on the lines of figures, like a rope of rescue, I strove to make good my father's destruction, I strove and strove, and in due course was given the district of Sligo where I was to harvest the policies. Every quarter I would take the train to Sligo, trying to convince them to make their futures secure, but no, most of them had barely shillings for meat. And mean bitter little low people they seemed to me, all kin in my mind to the bully of Ballina, and often and often I thought of the three lost farms, and the farmer I ought to have been, harvesting the old acres of wheat in the majestic peace of a Roscommon autumn. But by dint of long work and a sober mind, Mai-Mai, I prospered and all was well. You come from people who always had a boat to row across the dark waters of the Irish story.

OVER THE RIVER AND THROUGH THE WOODS

BY JOE DiPIETRO

FRANK GIANELLI — Nick's maternal grandfather, 80 years old.

SYNOPSIS: Nick is a single, Italian-American guy from New Jersey. His parents retired and moved to Florida. That doesn't mean his family isn't still in Jersey. In fact, he sees both sets of his grandparents every Sunday for dinner. This is routine until he has to tell them that he's been offered a dream job. The job he's been waiting for — marketing executive — would take him away from his beloved, but annoying, grandparents. He tells them. The news doesn't sit so well. Thus begins a series of schemes to keep Nick around. How could he betray his family's love to move to Seattle for a job, wonder his grandparents? Well, Frank, Aida, Nunzio and Emma do their level best, and that includes bringing to dinner the lovely — and single — Caitlin O'Hare as bait, but will they be able to get him to stay?

FRANK. You know the problem with old stories, Nick? You tell them and you realize that people don't change, people do the same things over and over again. When I was a little boy, every Christmas morning, on the cobblestones in town, there would appear this — this sea of vendors — their carts covered with toys — and what I remember most, is the colors — bright reds and blues and oranges — like a rainbow of toys. And my father would carry me in his arms and take me to the first cart, and he'd point to some tiny, dark toy, while I'd point to the biggest and most colorful, but my father would shake his head "no" and we'd move on to the next. And I'd point to another beautiful toy, and he'd shake his head again, and we'd move on. And we'd do that again and again until we had gone to each cart. And then he'd buy me some little gray toy I barely wanted, and I'd start crying, and he'd carry me back into our house. I always resented him for that — hated him for that. And when I was fourteen, my father put me on a boat to America and said, "Good-bye, that's where you're gonna live." I was fourteen. I hated him for that, too. Not long after that, he got tangled in a fishing net that was being thrown in the water, and his head hit the side of the boat and they never found him. Eight years from the day he sent me away, I returned to my hometown so my mother and sisters could meet my new family. It was during the holidays, and on Christmas morning, I took your mother in my arms and carried her outside and there they were — all the vendors, like they never left — with all their blue and red and beautiful toys. And your mother pointed to the brightest and prettiest, and any one she'd point at, I bought for her. And when we came back in, our arms full with this — this rainbow of toys, my mother took one look and said: "That's what your father wished he could do! But we barely had enough to buy food on Christmas. That's why he had to send you away. So you could make for yourself a life he could never give you." I always thought my father was a bastard who wouldn't give me anything. Turns out — he was giving me all he had.

PRELUDE TO A CRISIS

BY ARI ROTH

TEACHER — a professor at a major state university in the Midwest.

SYNOPSIS: A traveling teacher up for reappointment becomes obsessed by a student's "glistening brown lip-gloss" and, for the first time in his marriage and career, contemplates giving in to temptation. She invites herself up to his hotel room, ostensibly in need of special instruction, and brings along her laptop. He presses her cursor. Together they scroll through her incendiary new story as the flirtation of earlier office-hour banter gives way to sobering reality when the student becomes the bearer of some destabilizing news. She leaves. He knows he has a crisis to report home to his wife.

TEACHER. I'm gonna say something and it's gonna smack of defensiveness but that's what I am these days — I am a wall of it. I am the Berlin Wall of Confidence. And so what if it's unappealing? I'd pre*fer* me as confident. I'd prefer me employed. Which I may not be. Not up to me. What's up to me is my conscience and I've decided to come out about it so here goes ...

I forgot what I was gonna say. I-was-gonna-*say*-something; it-was-gonna-smack-of-defensiveness-but-that's-what-I-*am*; I am a *wall* ... I honestly hate this device. I'm forever telling my students how much I hate this kind of device! Man alone, in a room, wondering a*loud* whether some pixie of an honors student is ever gonna show — OK, there ... I gave a very promising honors student my room number about three hours ago. And I'm up for reappointment. I'm gonna start over. *(Clears throat. A different tack; cheerful.)*

I'm assuming this isn't done. I've certainly never done this! I've only *imagined* giving an honors student my room number, and now *acting* upon it, I take it as a sign of Growth; and Strength; and Maturity; or Stupidity; could be that.

Actually, it's not even the room number; it's the extension, but they're the same and she can figure it out — "Either call or come by." That's how we left it. Apparently, my hotel is on the way back to the *sorority,* so … Um, she's not really an honors student. I just made that up to look better; or feel better, which is truly insane, given how I anticipate feeling at the end of this interlude. Not that I have any *experience* with these kinds of interludes. Or more accurately, I barely … "Either call or come by." That's how we left it. Big reading tomorrow. End-of-term presentations. That's why I'm staying over — that, and a quickie with the Chair — meeting — about next year. Haven't heard, but not to worry. "All gonna sail though." That's what my wife says, but I mean, what does *she* really know? Which is an interesting question; or *the* interesting question, given what I'm doing here; that I've actually bought a bottle of *Fetzer Merlot* — I don't even drink Merlot! But maybe she *does* know; my wife; about the job; and I'll keep it; which is needed. Extremely needed. Given our situation — a gig like this is a gift! You wanna hold onto it. Not fuck it up! Not invite some pixie-of-an-honors-student-who's-not-even-an-honors-student up for drinks or anything boneheaded, which I didn't. *Her* suggestion. I think that's important to establish; that she was nervous about her climax. That's what she said, half-smiling, in that flirty, office-hour banter we sometimes get into.

PROOF

BY DAVID AUBURN

ROBERT — 50s, a mathematician.

SYNOPSIS: On the eve of her twenty-fifth birthday, Catherine, a troubled young woman, has spent years caring for her brilliant but unstable father, Robert, a famous mathematician. Now, following his death, she must deal with her own volatile emotions; the arrival of her estranged sister, Claire; and the attentions of Hal, a former student of her father's who hopes to find valuable work in the 103 notebooks that her father left behind. Over the long weekend that follows, a burgeoning romance and the discovery of a mysterious notebook draw Catherine into the most difficult problem of all: How much of her father's madness — or genius — will she inherit?

ROBERT. [...] This is the time of year when you don't want to be tied down to anything. You want to be outside. I love Chicago in September. Perfect skies. Sailboats on the water. Cubs losing. Warm, the sun still hot ... with the occasional blast of Arctic wind to keep you on your toes, remind you of winter. Students coming back, bookstores full, everybody busy.

I was in a bookstore yesterday. Completely full, students buying books ... browsing ... Students do a hell of a lot of browsing, don't they? Just browsing. You see them shuffling around with their backpacks, goofing off, taking up space. You'd call it loitering except every once in a while they pick up a book and flip the pages: "browsing." I admire it. It's an honest way to kill an afternoon. In the back of a used bookstore, or going through a crate of somebody's old record albums — not looking for anything, just looking, what the hell, touching the old book jackets, seeing what somebody threw out, seeing what they underlined ... maybe you find something great, like an old thriller with a painted cover from the '40s, or a textbook one of your professors used when he was a student — his name is written in it very carefully ... Yeah, I like it. I like watching the students. Wondering what they're gonna buy, what they're gonna read. What kind of ideas they'll come up with when they settle down and get to work ...

I'm not doing much right now. It does get harder. It's a stereotype that happens to be true, unfortunately for me — unfortunately for you, for all of us.

THE RIDE DOWN MOUNT MORGAN

BY ARTHUR MILLER

LYMAN — a successful middle-aged man.

SYNOPSIS: Lyman's desires have allowed him to believe that loving — and marrying — two women at the same time is the kind of love that is totally truthful, and that he is being true to himself. When found out, his wives, Theo and the younger Leah, clarify the position: Only by deceiving everyone at the same time has he found a way to his own false sense of truth. While lying in the hospital, recovering from bad injuries after a car crash, Lyman's wives meet. They are shocked and devastated, as are the children who once adored Lyman, and now verge on despising him. As we follow the chain of events that lead up to this day, what is revealed is a selfish man, willing to take, while others around him are willing to give and to turn a blind's eye to suspicions. We also feel the indictment of a society that urges us to give meaning to our life by individually defining it only for ourselves. In the end, Lyman is left by those who once loved him, and he must face the loneliness he now knows is his real, true self.

LYMAN. Is that the regret you end up with? ... Shit, that was cruel, Tom, forgive me, will you? Damnit, why do I let myself get depressed? It's all pointless guilt, that's all! Here I start from nothing, create forty-two hundred jobs for people, and raise over sixty ghetto blacks to office positions when that was not easy to do — I should be proud of myself, son of a bitch! I am! I am! *(He bangs on the desk, then subsides, looks front and downward.)* I love your view. That red river of taillights gliding down. Park Avenue on a winter's, night — and all those silky white thighs crossing inside

91

those heated limousines ... Christ — can there be a sexier vision in, the world? I keep thinking of my father — how connected he was to his life; couldn't wait to open the store every morning and happily count the pickles, rearrange the olive barrels. People like that knew the main thing. Which is what? What is the main thing, do you know? — Look, don't worry, I really can't imagine myself without Theodora, she's a great, great wife! ... I love that woman! It's always good talking to you, Tom. *(Starts to go, halts.)* Maybe it's simply that if you try to live according to your real desires, you have to end up looking like a shit.

ROMANCE IN D

BY JAMES SHERMAN

CHARLES NORTON — a musician, 40.

SYNOPSIS: ROMANCE IN D takes place in two side-by-side apartments in present-day Chicago. Charles Norton, a musicologist, lives in one apartment alone with his books and music. Isabel Fox, a poet on the verge of a divorce, moves into the other apartment and puts her head in the oven in a half-baked suicide attempt. Charles, next door, smells the gas and inadvertently becomes Isabel's savior. George Fox, Isabel's father, comes to town and tries to cheer her up. Helen Norton, Charles' mother, encourages Charles to get to know Isabel, but Charles refuses to become involved. Isabel makes the effort to befriend Charles and he, try as he may to resist, falls in love. One day, when Charles and Isabel are away, Helen and George meet and they discover that they have their own similar interests. Will Helen and George fall in love and leave the children to fend for themselves? Will Charles profess his love for Isabel and risk another heartbreak? Will Isabel go back to her husband or put her head back in the oven? All four characters use their knack for music and words as they nervously navigate the path of true love.

CHARLES. I bought lox and bagels. Would you like some lox and bagel?
[ISABEL. No.]
CHARLES. All right. I don't want to disturb you. I don't want to invade your space. I'll just, um ... eat. *(He takes out a bagel.)* You know ... You might find this interesting. You notice how I say, "lox and bagel"? Most people say, "bagels and lox," but think about it. Lox — no matter where you go — is eighteen, nineteen dollars a pound. Bagels are — well, they're not exactly a dime a

93

dozen, but they're only about five dollars for a dozen. So given the relative merits of an insignificant lump of dough versus a thinly sliced treasure of fine smoked salmon … Why should the bagel get top billing? Huh? I ask you. *(No response.)* Which leads me to my second point. Why say "bagels and lox" as if the whole point of the exercise is to taste a bagel? It's the lox I want. So this is what I do. *(He demonstrates as he talks.)* First of all, I never slice a bagel. I could slice through and cut that little fleshy part between my thumb and forefinger. So I just take the bagel and rip it in half. *(He does so. He takes out a container of cream cheese.)* Now, the cream cheese. You'll notice … I don't use cream cheese. *(He tosses the cream cheese on the counter.)* You see the way people pile on the cream cheese? It makes me sick. It's a condiment! Most people, I could say, "Here's some bagel and lox," give them just a bagel with a mound of cream cheese on it, and they wouldn't even notice the lox was missing. *(He unwraps the lox.)* So now, the pièce de résistance. I don't shove the lox between two halves of a bagel. *(He breaks off a hunk of a bagel.)* I take a piece of a bagel and wrap the lox around it. *(He does so.)* Getting the full flavor of the lox. And full value for my delicatessen dollar. Voilà. *(He holds it up.)* Jewish sushi.

ST NICHOLAS

BY CONOR McPHERSON

A MAN — late 50s.

SYNOPSIS: ST NICHOLAS finds an aging, jaded theatre critic recounting his obsession with a young actress, and how that obsession leads to a journey into a macabre world of vampires from which he almost can't escape.

MAN.
When I was a boy, I was afraid of the dark ... What was there.
And maybe one of the things I thought was there was vampires.
I don't know. I can't remember now.
But like all of us, whatever idea I did have about them, it was probably all the superstitious bullshit we get in books. And fiction. But that was nothing like the real thing. Like anything, the real thing is a lot more ordinary.
It's a "matter of fact." Matter of fact.
And that's far more frightening than anything you can make up.
Because it's real.
It's just there. Casual as everything else. Just waiting to be dealt with.
And there are practical things to be learned. Yes indeed.
Back in those days I was a fat bastard.
And I had a big red mush from drinking.
This is back before I met the vampires.
Before I knew what power was and what evil was.
But back then I thought I knew everything.
And I had lots of what I thought power was.
Because I was a theatre critic.
I was a journalist. I was a lucky bastard. I was blessed, or cursed,

whichever, with the ability to string words together. I could string words together.

And that's all it was.

I mean, I was intelligent, but I had no real thoughts about things.

I'd never taken the care to form an opinion. I just had them.

And only one care in the world, when I think back on it now, me.

I wanted ... everything.

Love, I suppose. Respect. Esteem.

But I didn't deserve it. No, I don't think I deserved any respect. But I got it.

Oh yeah. I got it. Because people were afraid of me. I loved it.

SIDE MAN

BY WARREN LEIGHT

JONESY — male, late 20s to early 60s. A one-eyed, prophetic, junkie trombone player.

SYNOPSIS: Set in 1953 and traveling to 1985, the play unfolds through the eyes of Clifford, the only son of Gene, a jazz trumpet player, and Terry, an alcoholic mother. Alternating between their New York City apartment and a smoke-filled music club, Clifford narrates the story of his broken family and the decline of jazz as popular entertainment. Gene's music career on the big band circuit ultimately crumbles with the advent of Elvis and rock 'n' roll. Terry begs him to get a nine-to-five job to support the family, but Gene refuses to enter the "straight world" of regular paychecks, mortgages and security. For Gene, who knows jazz better than his own son, music is not just a job; it's his life. Their marriage slowly dissolves and young Clifford is witness to it all. As things worsen, Clifford assumes the role of parent and throws the hopeless Gene out of his mother's apartment. When an adult Clifford visits Gene in a rundown jazz club after years of separation, he requests that the old man play his mother's favorite song, the old standard "Why Was I Born?" Clifford then asks, "Dad, why was I born?" It becomes Clifford's last, heartbreaking plea for his father's love.

JONESY. I'm all fucked up, Gene.
[GENE. What the hell happened?]
JONESY. They wanted me to tell them who my dealer was. They said we'll give you a fix, if you tell us where you cop. They waved it in front of my face. I was dying for it. But I said, i can't trust you guys. Let me fix myself up first, then I'll tell you where I cop. So the bastards give me my stash, they'd already taken half of it for themselves, but I tie off, I shoot up, and I'm feeling no pain. OK

wiseass, they say, tell us where this heroin comes from? I look them right in the eye and I tell them the truth: *(Pause.)* General MacArthur. *[(Gene looks at Jonesy, shakes his head.)]* Well, how the hell do you think this stuff gets into the country? Anyway, this fuckin' bull goes nuts. He smacks me across the face. The other guys let him whale on me for a while before they pulled him off. *(Jonesy opens his mouth, shows Gene his teeth.)* He broke three of my teeth, Gene. *(Starts to cry.)* I don't know if I'll ever be able to play.

SNAKEBIT

BY DAVID MARSHALL GRANT

JONATHAN — 30s, an actor.

SYNOPSIS: A study of modern friendship when put to the test, the play centers on Jonathan and his wife Jenifer while they visit their oldest friend, Michael, at his home in Los Angeles. Jonathan, an actor, is in L.A. auditioning for a film — his first big break at stardom — and he's dragged Jenifer with him for support. Jenifer is distant because their daughter was left at home with a relative and she's become ill. Michael is distracted since his boyfriend has left him and one of the children he counsels was beaten and put in a hospital where he cannot see her. At first the focus is on the universal questions we all face at one point or another, specifically self-doubt and our selfish need for support. With the arrival of a guest, the play becomes deeper and forces us to see how ugly we can be when we look only at ourselves when we really should remember to look at others — especially those we love.

JONATHAN.   The last time? *(Beat.)* All right, I don't think any of this is a problem. Okay? I think this has all been built up in your mind and before we all have a heart attack here, I think we should just call. So give me the number.
[JENIFER.   I'm waiting for Michael. I have to.]
JONATHAN.   *(Trying not to explode.)* Jesus fucking Christ, Jenny. You know, I'm trying to do the right thing here, but you are making this almost impossible. I'm holding on to us by nothing. Do you understand? By less than nothing.
[JENIFER.   If you want to stay here —]
JONATHAN.   This is my family! I'm about to snap. Really I am. *(Trying to remain calm.)* Yes I want to stay here. I want you to call. That's what I want you to do. I just want you and I to make this

call together. I'm your husband. Michael is not your husband. You had no right to sleep with him, Jenny. God damn you, it's just completely faithless.

[JENIFER. Jonathan, please stop it.]

JONATHAN. *(Exploding.)* NO, YOU STOP IT, I'M NOT DOING ANYTHING! OKAY? YOU'RE THE ONE WHO FUCKED HIM! I DIDN'T FUCK HIM! YOU FUCKED HIM! YOU WERE FUCKING MY BEST FRIEND, JENIFER! THREE MONTHS BEFORE OUR WEDDING. FUCK YOU! THAT'S COMPLETELY UNBELIEVABLE. HE'S MY BEST FRIEND. FUCK YOU! I COULD BE DEAD RIGHT NOW! FUCK YOU!

STUPID KIDS

BY JOHN C. RUSSELL

JOHN "NEECHEE" CRAWFORD — 17, lonely, angry, queer.

SYNOPSIS: In rapid, highly stylized, music video–like scenes, STUPID KIDS follows four students at Joe McCarthy High School as they make their way from first through eighth period and beyond, struggling with the fears, frustrations and longings peculiar to youth. Jim is the new guy in town, sexy, a rebel. Judy is the popular blonde cheerleader. Neechee and Kimberly are the resident outcasts, both of whom are secretly gay. Will Jim become popular? Will Judy give her virginity to Jim? Will Neechee and Kimberly confess they're gay? With his magical touch, John C. Russell turns these familiar stereotypes into deeply moving and provocative archetypes of adolescence whose jocular lingo takes on a lyricism that is both true to its source and astonishingly revelatory of the hearts and minds of contemporary youth.

NEECHEE.   Dear Stranger,
    I am alone inside myself. I am a lone loner lonely alone inside myself inside this school inside this town inside this state inside this society inside this world. I look out cuz in is too tiny — I look out and I see you. I see you alone, a lone loner lonely, looking out, looking for something real. Your eyes have extra penetration — you can make people like you. Strength and pride glow out of your eyes and saturate them, the ones that don't wanna know. They can't resist your power. And try as I may, I can't resist, myself. I fall limp and winded at your proverbial feet, ready to fuck anarchy and free will and just do your bidding. Your eyes — *(He can't really fathom having written this.)*
    Your eyes blind me and I forget all logic, I wipe all the rules out of my brain. I can, in a tiny place inside myself, inside my lone

101

loner lonely self, I can love you. But then the world makes its petty demands. It makes me leave myself, leave your eyes and speak words, so then I follow the rules and do what you tell me and try to act like we're both just regular joes. But sometimes I get lost in your eyes, so lost. Can't find my way out.

Yours always,

THIS DAY AND AGE

BY NAGLE JACKSON

TONY — late 20s; Marjorie's son.

SYNOPSIS: Affluent, newly widowed and wonderfully politically incorrect, Marjorie is enjoying life sitting by her pool, having imaginary conversations with her late husband, Jack, when both her grown-up children come calling: Ann with her British husband, Brian, and Tony with his Asian-American wife, Joy — an ex-ballet dancer. Neither sibling knows the other has the same plan: to come home and live with poor old Mom. When Marjorie's succinct reply is "no," they can't believe it. Not only does she not want them living there but — she has decided to sell the estate and move to New Zealand. Family chaos ensues. Sibling rivalry reaches alarming proportions; brother-in-law begins to lust after sister-in-law, and even the water in the pool turns murky. Eventually Marjorie has an epiphany — including a visitation from her deceased husband, songwriter Jack, who urges her to "let 'em go, let 'em all go." Her decision, which has nothing to do with New Zealand, takes everyone by surprise and gives her a new freedom and a new life.

TONY. I don't know why I come back. Lots of us are doing that.
[MARJORIE. Us?]
TONY. My friends. My generation. Going back to hometowns. Going back to school. Just going back. 'Cause there's nothing else.
[MARJORIE. Nonsense.]
TONY. No. It's true. It's all been done. The agenda. Brave New World. Pushed to the sea both East and West. People go to California and jump off the Golden Gate Bridge or O.D. on drugs. Or they go home, "Uncle!" … "I give!" … "King's X" … Just let me come home, Mom. I can't do anything. We'll help out. Joy is great at everything. The kids are good. They really are. We'll

do everything for you. You can … you can just *bask*. In the sun.
[…]
TONY. Mom, I can't do it. I can't make it. There's nothing to
make. I do the New York thing, the commute thing. I do lunch
and all that other crap, and my mind isn't even there. I'm somewhere else. I don't know what people are saying to me half the
time. When I left the School of Design, I had a kind of vague
agenda. But there's nothing there. There are thousands of design-
ers. Who gives a shit? Who gives a good goddamn about *design*
when we're all just treading water. Nothing's happening. The street
is jammed with people running every which way. And nothing's
happening. Nothing at all. I am such a disappointment to you. I
know that. God, it's terrible to know that.

THIS IS OUR YOUTH

BY KENNETH LONERGAN

DENNIS ZIEGLER — 21 years old.

SYNOPSIS: In 1982, on Manhattan's Upper West Side, the wealthy, articulate pot-smoking teenagers who were small children in the '60s have emerged as young adults in a country that has just resoundingly rejected everything they were brought up to believe in. The very last wave of New York City's '60s-style liberalism has come of age — and there's nowhere left to go. In meticulous, hilarious and agonizing detail, THIS IS OUR YOUTH follows forty-eight hours of three very lost young souls in the big city at the dawn of the Reagan Era: Warren Straub, a dejected nineteen-year-old who steals fifteen-thousand dollars from his abusive lingerie-tycoon father; Dennis Ziegler, the charismatic domineering drug-dealing friend who helps him put the money to good use; and Jessica Goldman, the anxiously insightful young woman Warren yearns for.

DENNIS. I just can't believe this, man, it's like so completely bizarre. And it's not like I even liked the guy that much, you know? I just *knew* him. You know? But if we had been doing those speedballs last night we could both be *dead* now. Do you understand how *close* that is? I mean ... It's *death*. *Death.* It's so incredibly heavy, it's like so much heavier than like ninety-five percent of the shit you deal with in the average day that constitutes your supposed life, and it's like so totally off to the *side* it's like completely ridiculous. I mean that was *it*. That was his *life*. Period. The Life of Stuart. A fat Jew from Long Island with a grotesque accent who sold drugs and ate steak and did nothing of note like whatsoever. I don't know, man. I'm like, high on fear. I feel totally high on fear. I'm like — I don't even know what to *do* with myself. I wanna like go to *cooking* school in *Florence,* or like go into *show* business. I could so totally be a completely great chef it's like ridiculous. Or like an actor or like a director. I should totally direct movies, man, I'd be a genius at it. Like if you take the average person with the average sensibility or sense of humor or the way they look at the world and what thoughts they have or what they think, and you compare it to the way *I* look at shit and the shit I come up with to *say,* or just the *slant* I put on shit, there's just like no comparison at all. I could totally make movies, man, I would be like one of the greatest movie makers of all time. Plus I am like so much better at sports than anyone I know except Wally and those big black basketball players, man, but I totally played with those guys and completely earned their respect, and Wally was like, "Denny, man, you are the only white friend I have who I can take uptown and hang out with my friends and not be *embarrassed.*" Because I just go up there and hang out with them and like get them so much more stoned than they've ever been in their *life* and like am completely not intimidated by them at *all.* You know?

THE UNEASY CHAIR

BY EVAN SMITH

CAPTAIN JOSIAH WICKETT — a retired military man.

SYNOPSIS: Somewhere in the nineteenth century, Amelia Pickles, a prim and proper spinster of modest means, agrees to let out a room in her Victorian London establishment to a retired military man, Josiah Wickett. The arrangement seems to be working out until Mr. Wickett decides to play matchmaker with Miss Pickles' prissy niece Alexandrina, and his nephew, Darlington, an officer in the cavalry. Through a gross misinterpretation, Miss Pickles believes she, not Alexandrina, is the object of Mr. Wickett's, not Darlington's, affection. Miss Pickles is convinced Mr. Wickett will soon ask for her hand in marriage. When he denies, she decides to take her boarder to a court of law for breach of promise. Mr. Wickett loses the trial. Or does he win? He doesn't wish to pay Miss Pickles her settlement and instead he opts to marry the lonely woman. Through the musings, regrets, anecdotes and comedic bickerings between their forced duet it seems as though just maybe they were meant to be together after all.

WICKETT. She was a kindred spirit. A soul mate. And here began one of the most blissful periods I have known in my life. I recall one evening in my first month of residency, one detail of which will serve to indicate the depth and breadth of this amazing woman's intuition of what is correct and comfortable. We were both seated in the parlour. I was reading; she was sewing. Together, as it were, in the same room, respectful, considerate, but separate, distinct entities, under no obligation one to the other, secure and content. Those who know only hot passion and its opposite, loneliness, cannot dream of the satisfaction in a cool and distant intimacy, for intimacy it is, made more intimate by the coolness and distance. Then, on that night: *(He coughs.)* Nine landladies out of ten, nay, nine-hundred-and-ninety-nine landladies out of a thousand would have remarked that cough, asked how I felt, was I cold, was I warm, was I catching something; reasonable inquiries, all, but requiring a reply which would lead to conversation, and which would have required a feigned interest in the other's health from that moment forward, irrevocably. All silence and comfort is lost forever. Miss Pickles, however, said nothing. I felt for her in that moment a cool and distant regard that I believe is as truly and deeply felt as the hottest passion ever imagined by a lady novelist.

THE VAST DIFFERENCE

BY JEFF DANIELS

GEORGE NOONAN — a flight attendant, 30s.

SYNOPSIS: George Noonan needs a vasectomy. As a flight attendant and the father of five girls, George turns a routine visit to his urologist into a psychotherapy session about life, the insignificance of the modern-day man and the vast difference between stewards and stewardesses.

GEORGE. [...] Have you ever been to Hollywood, sir?
[EDWARDS.   No, I haven't.]
GEORGE.   There's this movie theatre out there. Very famous. And in the sidewalk, as you walk into this place, they've got imprints of all the hands and feet of all the biggest movie stars in history.
[EDWARDS.   I've heard of it, yes.]
GEORGE.   Everywhere you look, pair after pair of famous hands and famous feet. Gable and Lombard, Tracy and Hepburn, Bette Davis, Joan Crawford, Gary Cooper, Charlton Heston and, of course, the one I came all that way to see, The Duke.
[EDWARDS.   John Wayne.]
GEORGE.   *[Right.]* My father's favorite movie hero. The epitome of a Man's Man. There he was, right in the center, right there in the middle of all of them. All the other stars' squares seemed to retreat, seemed to step back. Make way for The Duke. Maybe it was by design. Maybe The Duke wouldn't agree to do it otherwise, I don't know. It didn't matter. I got down on my hands and knees. Just like this. Never forget it. *(George gets down on his hands and knees.)*
[EDWARDS.   George.]
GEORGE.   Hang with me now. I put my hands out. Just like this. And there in front of me was the imprint of the hands of the man who in my estimation was the greatest living male figure of

the twentieth century. All that is strong, all that is brave, true, courageous — everything every ordinary man could ever hope to be was right there in those ten fingers and two palms immortalized in crushed stone and mortar. I reached out. And I slowly let my hands become one with his. It sounds sexual I know, maybe it was, I don't care, I went with it. And as I knelt there, our hands together in cement, I stopped in my tracks. And his tracks. Tears welled up in my eyes. I couldn't believe what I was seeing. What I was feeling. But it was true. John Wayne's hands were smaller than mine. The Duke had small hands.

VERNON EARLY

BY HORTON FOOTE

VERNON EARLY — 50s, thin, a doctor.

SYNOPSIS: VERNON EARLY revisits American life in Horton Foote's fictional town of Harrison, Texas, during the 1950s. The title character, Vernon, is a doctor, in the days when the house call was commonplace. Consumed by his work, his spirit has been eroded by the pressures of his job and the lingering depression he shares with his wife, Mildred, over the loss of their adopted child to his birth mother. Mirroring the tragic existence of the Earlys, many of Harrison's other residents are also consumed with the self-inflicted wounds of life: aging, individual isolation, love and racial inequality. Through all of the bleakness of life there still shines a glimmer of hope reflected in the spirit of the town's sad doctor: Vernon Early.

VERNON. If I passed him on the street I doubt I'd even recognize him. Of course, he wouldn't know me from Adam.
[...]
VERNON. I tell you that was a terrible day when the agency called just a month before the adoption became final and said the mother had changed her mind and wanted the boy back.
[REENIE. Why did she change her mind?]
VERNON. Well, she'd had the baby without her mother's knowing it, and then just before the legal time was up, her grandmother died and the girl got stricken by remorse during the wake and confessed to her mother what she had done and the mother went to the boy that got her daughter pregnant and made him marry her daughter and then they went to the agency and asked for the baby back and the agency called me, and said it was their legal right to do so, but I decided to take it to court and I spent a

fortune let me tell you fighting for him in the courts. I finally went to the girl and her mother and offered her $50,000 if she would let us keep the baby. *(A pause.)* But no. No way. The day we gave him back it was like a funeral. Mildred cried for months. I never thought I would get over the hurt, but I did, of course, I did. That was almost the hardest thing I had to get over. Almost.

THE WEIR

BY CONOR McPHERSON

JACK — 50s.

SYNOPSIS: In a bar in rural Ireland, the local men swap spooky stories in an attempt to impress Valerie, a young woman from Dublin who recently moved into a nearby "haunted" house. However, the tables are soon turned when she tells them a chilling story of her own.

JACK. I had a girl. A lovely girl back then. We were courting for three, years, and em … 1963 to 66. But she wanted to go up to Dublin, you know. She would have felt that's what we should have done. And I don't know why it was a thing with me that I … an irrational fear, I suppose, that kept me here. And I couldn't understand why she wanted to be running off up to Dublin, you know? And she did in the end, anyway, like. And she was working up there waiting for me to come.

But with me it was a mad thing, that I thought it was a thousand fucking miles away. Hated going up.

I went up a few times like. But … I was going up for … you know … she had a room. A freezing, damp place. I was a terrible fella. It became that that was the only thing I was going for. I couldn't stand being away. I don't know why. Ah, I'd be all excited about going up for the physical … the freedom of it. But after a day and a night, and I'd had my fill, we'd be walking in the park and I'd be all catty and bored, and moochy. *(Pause.)*

Breaking the poor girl's heart. Ah, you get older and look back on why you did things, you see that a lot of the time, there wasn't a reason. You do a lot of things out of pure cussedness.

I stopped answering her letters. And I'd fucking dread one coming to the house. And her in it wondering how I was and was

113

there something wrong with the post or this. *(Pause.)*

I can't explain what carry on I was up to. I had just ... left her out. Being the big fella, me dad handing over the business to me. Me swanning around. A man of substance. And then I had the gall to feel resentful when she wrote and said she was getting married to a fella. *(Pause.)*

And I was all that it was her fault for going up in the first place. Tss.

THE YOUNG GIRL AND THE MONSOON

BY JAMES RYAN

HANK — 38, youthful, attractive and vulnerable, yet very private.

SYNOPSIS: *Growing up is hard to do—particularly if you are a pre-adolescent girl in Manhattan living with a photo-journalist father reeling from a messy divorce. Constance is a thirteen-year-old torn by life and stretched between parents, struggling through those daunting rites of passage which none of us finds easy. Things aren't all smooth-sailing for her father, Hank, who is attempting to provide an anchor for Constance, while also working to get his own life into some kind of order, especially regarding his recent serious relationship with a younger woman, Erin, twenty-six. If Constance has only Hank for guidance, then Hank only has Giovanna, thirty-eight, a tempestuous colleague and genuine friend, with whom Hank has an off-and-on (chiefly off) affair. This romantic comedy turns on Hank's efforts to find enough room in his life for both Constance and Erin, and achieve the balance and maturity that have, so far, eluded him.*

HANK. I was at a briefing and a General is showing some videos and before he turns them on he says, "I'm going to show you the luckiest man in Iraq today. Keep your eye on the crosshairs." And the world sees a guy running across a bridge as a rocket is heading right for him. He runs off the screen just as the bridge blows up. Everyone in the room laughs. Including me.

Eight hours later I get into Baghdad and I've got two hours to get some pictures. I get to that bridge and there was that guy. He'd been left overnight. His body parts were scattered about.

So I snap away. Then comes time for the write-up. There's this kid, a twelve-year-old-girl, staring at me. I asked her all sorts of questions, had the interpreter work overtime. No matter what I would say, the kid would say yes to it. I bet you went to a lot of places with your daddy? And the interpreter would say yes. I bet he taught you how to swim. Yes. I bet he probably saved your life one time because you went over your head, too deep in the water. And she'd say yes. I bet the night he died he was at this bridge because he heard that there may be some people in danger and he was there to get them to safety and when he showed up there was no one there and then he got hit. And she said yes. It was ridiculous. The silliest story I ever wrote.

Later that day I found out that this girl was really the daughter of that man. The guy cut in half, in front of us. And that she was in such shock that she would have said yes to anything, did anything anyone told her and that I sullied that somehow, I had belittled what was really happening to her ... I felt she had been used by me somehow. You know?

[GIOVANNA. Yeah.]

HANK. These thoughts. These images, they come to me at night now. I'm in the Intercontinental Hotel in Paris and that throat being slit in El Salvador five years before appears to me and I wake up and scream bloody murder. All those things I observed, those traumas over the years, they seeped into me, I didn't expect that, and now they're oozing out.

Suddenly I and the image have merged. It no longer reflects me. It has become me. People are no longer personages, they're symbols, made into an explicable lie. And that's the most terrifying ring of hell, Giovanna, because when you become the lie, you're erased.

I lied, Giovanna, and now I'm getting a prize for it.

PERMISSIONS ACKNOWLEDGMENTS